Preface

Welcome to Your Python Journey!
Python is not just a programming language; it's a tool that can empower you to do amazing things—whether it's automating repetitive tasks, analyzing large sets of data, building your own website, or even creating your own artificial intelligence models. Python's versatility and ease of Use make it one of the most beloved programming languages in the world.

The Python Textbook aims to be your comprehensive guide on your Python programming journey. Whether you are a complete beginner or a seasoned developer looking to deepen your Python knowledge, we have something for everyone. With hands-on examples, real-world projects, and deep explorations of Python's features and capabilities, this book will serve as both a tutorial and a reference.

What This Book Covers?
Foundations: Learn the syntax, variables, and basic types that make up Python.
Control Structures: Master the art of decision-making and repetition with if-else statements and loops.
Data Structures: From lists and tuples to dictionaries and sets, understand how to effectively organize and manipulate data.
Functions and OOP: Gain a strong understanding of modularity, functions, and object-oriented programming.
Libraries and Frameworks: An introduction to the vast ecosystem of Python libraries, including NumPy for numerical operations, pandas for data manipulation, and frameworks like Django for web development.
Advanced Topics: Dive into topics like decorators, context managers, metaclasses, and asynchronous programming.

Table of Contents

Chapter 1

Introduction to Python

Python is a versatile and beginner-friendly programming language that has gained immense popularity for its simplicity and readability. It's straightforward syntax and dynamic typing make it easy to learn and use, making it an excellent choice for individuals new to programming. Python's core philosophy, often referred to as the "Zen of Python," emphasizes readability and a clean, elegant coding style. This is evident through its use of indentation for defining code blocks and the absence of semicolons. Python supports various data types, including integers, floats, strings, and booleans, and its dynamic nature allows variables to change types during runtime. Control structures like if-elif-else statements and loops (for and while) guide program flow, while functions enable modular and reusable code. Python's extensive standard library, along with numerous third-party libraries, facilitates tasks ranging from web development and data analysis to machine learning and automation. Overall, Python's user-friendly nature and wide range of applications make it an ideal starting point for aspiring programmers.

Python is a highly flexible and accessible programming language that has garnered widespread acclaim for its user-friendly design and code readability. Its uncluttered syntax and the lack of complex rules for structuring code make it an ideal choice for beginners venturing into the world of programming. One of the standout features of Python is its "Zen," a set of aphorisms that advocate for simplicity and clarity in code.

Python is dynamically typed, allowing developers to change variable types on the fly, which adds to its ease of use. Its control flow mechanisms, such as if-else conditions and loop constructs like while and for, are straightforward, aiding in intuitive program design. Functions in Python facilitate code reusability, and its object-oriented nature makes it apt for complex application development.

What sets Python apart is its enormous standard library that covers a wide array of tasks from file manipulation to network programming. Additionally, the language's ecosystem is enriched by an expansive range of third-party packages, which are instrumental in specialized fields likc data science, machine learning, and web application development.

In a nutshell, Python's clean syntax, comprehensive standard library, and its adaptability to various kinds of tasks make it a go-to language for developers of all skill levels.

1.1 What is Python?

Python is a high-level, readable programming language renowned for its versatility. It was created by Guido van Rossum in 1991 and has since gained immense popularity. Python's straightforward syntax makes it a favourite among beginners and experts, with a focus on readability through indentation. Its broad applications span web development, data analysis, AI, machine learning, and automation. The "Zen of Python" philosophy underlines its design principles, promoting clarity and simplicity. Python's rich standard library offers pre-built modules, further simplifying tasks. It's whitespace-driven structure enhances code consistency. Overall, Python's adaptability, readability, and active community contribute to its widespread usage and appeal.

The language is not just readable but also remarkably versatile, finding applications in various domains like web development, data analytics, artificial intelligence, and robotics. Python's expansive standard library offers modules for almost every conceivable task, making it a Swiss Army knife for programmers. The library's pre-existing modules make it easier for both newcomers and experienced coders to get things done efficiently.

One of Python's standout features is its consistency in structure, attributed to its use of whitespace and indentation, which standardizes the look and feel of code across projects. This, along with an active global community and a plethora of third-party libraries, makes Python a highly adaptive and ever-evolving language, suitable for both novices and experts alike.

1.2 History of Python

Python was conceived by Guido van Rossum in the late 1980s and its development started in December 1989. Python 0.9.0 was released in February 1991, marking its official debut. The language's name was inspired by the British comedy group Monty Python. Python 1.0 was released in January 1994 with new features and improved capabilities. Python 2.0, released in 2000, brought list comprehensions and Unicode support. The subsequent years saw Python gaining popularity due to its readability and versatility. Python 3.0, released in 2008, introduced significant changes, including a redesigned print function and improved Unicode support.

Despite initial resistance, Python 3 gradually gained adoption, leading to the coexistence of Python 2 and 3. In 2020, Python 2's official support ended, shifting focus entirely to Python 3.

Python's success can be attributed to its active community, vast standard library, and adoption by tech giants like Google and NASA. It's used in diverse fields, including web development, data science, AI, and more. Python's evolution continues, with frequent updates and improvements, solidifying its position as a prominent programming language.

1.3 Features of Python

Readable and Clear Syntax: Python's simple and clean syntax emphasizes code readability, making it easy for both beginners and experienced programmers to understand and maintain code.

Dynamic Typing: Python uses dynamic typing, allowing variables to change data types during runtime. This simplifies coding and makes the language more flexible.

Whitespace Indentation: Python uses indentation to define code blocks, eliminating the need for braces or semicolons. This enforces consistent formatting and enhances code clarity.

Large Standard Library: Python's extensive standard library offers a wide range of pre-built modules and functions that simplify various programming tasks, from file handling to web development.

Cross-Platform Compatibility: Python is available on various platforms, including Windows, macOS, and Linux, ensuring that code can run consistently across different systems.

Object-Oriented Programming (OOPs): Python supports object-oriented programming paradigms, allowing users to create reusable and structured code using classes and objects.

Interpreted Language: Python is an interpreted language, meaning that code is executed line by line by the interpreter. This enables quick development and testing without the need for compiling.

Extensive Third-Party Libraries: Python boasts a vast ecosystem of third-party libraries and frameworks that extend its capabilities, catering to different application domains such as web development (Django, Flask), data science (NumPy, Pandas), and more.

Community and Support: Python has a vibrant and active community of developers, providing resources, tutorials, and assistance to fellow programmers. This community-driven environment contributes to Python's growth and improvement.

Platform for Various Applications: Python is suitable for a wide range of applications, including web development, data analysis, scientific computing, artificial intelligence, machine learning, automation, and more.

Portability: Python code can be easily ported between different platforms due to its interpreted nature and cross-platform compatibility.

Scalability: While Python may not be as performant as some lower-level languages, it offers various ways to optimize and scale applications, including integration with compiled languages like C and using concurrency libraries.

1.4 Python Language Advantages and Application

Advantages of Python

Readable and Clear Syntax: Python's simple and clean syntax emphasizes code readability, making it easy for both beginners and experienced programmers to understand and maintain code.

Dynamic Typing: Python uses dynamic typing, allowing variables to change data types during runtime. This simplifies coding and makes the language more flexible.

Whitespace Indentation: Python uses indentation to define code blocks, eliminating the need for braces or semicolons. This enforces consistent formatting and enhances code clarity.

Large Standard Library: Python's extensive standard library offers a wide range of pre-built modules and functions that simplify various programming tasks, from file handling to web development.

Cross-Platform Compatibility: Python is available on various platforms, including Windows, macOS, and Linux, ensuring that code can run consistently across different systems.

Object-Oriented Programming (OOP): Python supports object-oriented programming paradigms, allowing users to create reusable and structured code using classes and objects.

Interpreted Language: Python is an interpreted language, meaning that code is executed line by line by the interpreter. This enables quick development and testing without the need for compiling.

Extensive Third-Party Libraries: Python boasts a vast ecosystem of third-party libraries and frameworks that extend its capabilities, catering to different application domains such as web development (Django, Flask), data science (NumPy, Pandas), and more.

Community and Support: Python has a vibrant and active community of developers, providing resources, tutorials, and assistance to fellow programmers. This community-driven environment contributes to Python's growth and improvement.

Platform for Various Applications: Python is suitable for a wide range of applications, including web development, data analysis, scientific computing, artificial intelligence, machine learning, automation, and more.

Portability: Python code can be easily ported between different platforms due to its interpreted nature and cross-platform compatibility.

Scalability: While Python may not be as performant as some lower-level languages, it offers various ways to optimize and scale applications, including integration with compiled languages like C and using concurrency libraries.

Disadvantages of Python

Performance: Python is an interpreted language, which can lead to slower execution speeds compared to compiled languages like C or C++.

Global Interpreter Lock (GIL): Python's GIL restricts the execution of multiple threads in a single process, limiting true parallelism in some cases.

Memory Consumption: Python's dynamic typing and memory management can lead to higher memory consumption compared to languages with more stringent memory control.

Not Ideal for Mobile Development: While Python can be used for mobile app development, it's not as commonly used as languages like Swift or Kotlin.

Limited in Mobile and Game Development: Python is less suitable for high-performance gaming or mobile apps that require resource-intensive operations.

Less Suitable for Low-Level Programming: Python's high-level nature makes it less suitable for low-level programming tasks like developing operating systems or device drivers.

Packaging and Distribution Challenges: Packaging and distributing Python applications can be challenging due to dependencies and version compatibility.

Limited Browser Support: While Python can be used for web development, it's not as commonly used for front-end web development compared to languages like JavaScript.

Applications Of Python

Web Development: Python is widely used for building dynamic and interactive websites. Frameworks like Django and Flask provide tools for rapid development, secure handling of user data, and efficient database management. Platforms like Instagram, Pinterest, and Spotify utilize Python for their backend web development.

Data Analysis and Visualization: Python's libraries such as Pandas, NumPy, and Matplotlib make it a popular choice for data analysis and visualization. Researchers, analysts, and data scientists use Python to clean, manipulate, and visualize data to extract valuable insights for decision-making. Companies like NASA and Netflix employ Python for data-driven insights.

Machine Learning and Artificial Intelligence: Python's libraries like TensorFlow, Keras, and scikit-learn empower developers and researchers to create machine learning models and AI applications. Python's flexibility and extensive libraries facilitate tasks such as image recognition, natural language processing, and recommendation systems. Applications like self-driving cars and voice assistants utilize Python-based AI.

Scientific Computing and Research:

Python is popular in scientific communities for tasks like simulations, numerical analysis, and complex mathematical computations. Libraries like SciPy and SymPy are used in research fields like physics, biology, and astronomy. The Large Hadron Collider at CERN uses Python for analyzing particle physics data.

Automation and Scripting:

Python's simplicity and readability make it an excellent choice for automating repetitive tasks and writing scripts. It's commonly used for tasks such as data scraping, file manipulation, and process automation. System administrators use Python to manage and automate server tasks, while content creators might automate social media posts.

1.5 Getting Started with Python

The programming language you will be learning is Python. Python is an example of a **high-level language**; other high-level languages you might have heard of are C++, PHP, and Java. As you might infer from the name high-level language, there are also **low-level languages**, sometimes referred to as machine languages or assembly languages. Loosely speaking, computers can only execute programs written in low-level languages. Thus, programs written in a high-level language have to be processed before they can run. This extra processing takes some time, which is a small disadvantage of high-level languages. However, the advantages to high-level languages are enormous.

First, it is much easier to program in a high-level language. Programs written in a high-level language take less time to write, they are shorter and easier to read, and they are more likely to be correct.

Second, high-level languages are **portable**, meaning that they can run on different kinds of computers with few or no modifications. Low-level programs can run on only one kind of computer and have to be rewritten to run on another.

Due to these advantages, almost all programs are written in high-level languages. Low-level languages are used only for a few specialized applications. Two kinds of programs process high-level languages into low-level languages: **interpreters** and **compilers**. An interpreter reads a high-level program and executes it, meaning that it does what the program says. It processes the program a little at a time, alternately reading lines and performing computations.

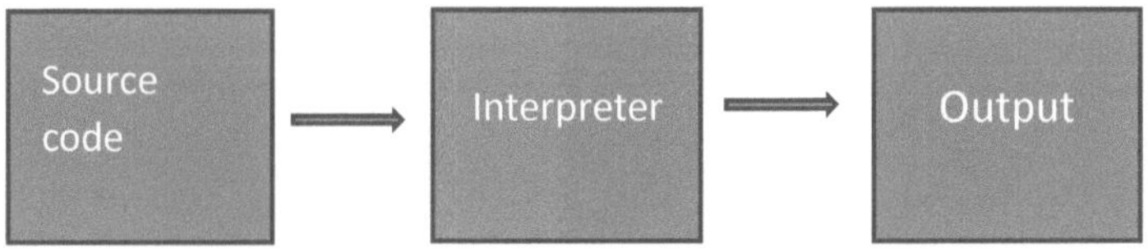

A compiler reads the program and translates it completely before the program starts running. In this case, the high-level program is called the **source code**, and the translated program is called the **object code** or the **executable**. Once a program is compiled, you can execute it repeatedly without further translation.

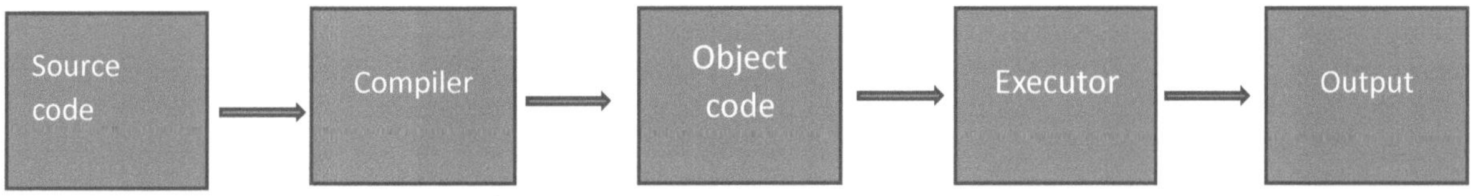

Many modern languages use both processes. They are first compiled into a lower level language, called **byte code**, and then interpreted by a program called a **virtual machine**. Python uses both processes, but because of the way programmers interact with it, it is usually considered an interpreted language.
For the core material in this book, you will not need to install or run Python natively on your computer. Instead, you'll be writing simple programs and executing them right in your browser.
At some point, you will find it useful to have a complete Python environment, rather than the limited environment available in this online textbook. To do that, you will either install Python on your computer so that it can run natively, or use a remote server that provides either a command line shell or a jupyter notebook environment.

1.5.1 Comments in Python

When you write code, it's important to explain why you're doing certain things in your script. This is where comments come in. Comments are like notes that you add to your code to help others (and yourself) understand what's going on. They're especially useful when you're dealing with complex ideas, formulas, or steps.
When you run your code, the computer ignores the comments completely. It only pays attention to the actual code and follows the instructions you've written. So, comments are just there to help humans understand the code better, while the computer doesn't pay any attention to them. Python employs three types of comments: single-line comments, multi-line comments, and documentation strings. By incorporating comments into code, developers can enhance its comprehensibility and aid others in understanding the code's purpose and functionality.

Types of comments in Python

- **Single-Line Comment:**

Single-line comments are used to explain a single line of code. They start with the # symbol and continue until the end of the line.
Example:

```
# This is a single-line comment explaining the purpose of the following line
age = 25  # Save the user's age.
```

- **Multi-Line Comment:**

Multi-line comments are used to explain larger sections of code. They are enclosed within triple quotes (''' or """) and can span multiple lines.
Example:

```
'''
This is a multi-line comment explaining
the process of calculating the average.
```

```
'''
total = 0
count = 0
for num in numbers:
    total += num
    count += 1
average = total / count
```

- **Documentation String (Docstring):**

Docstrings are used to provide documentation for functions, classes, modules, and methods. They are enclosed within triple quotes and can be accessed using the help() function or various documentation tools.

Example:

```
def calculate_square(num):
    """
    This function calculates the square of a given number
    :param num: The input number.
    :return: The square of the input number.
    """
    return num ** 2
```

These comments help explain the code's intent and functionality, making it easier for developers to understand and work with the code, especially when collaborating or revisiting the code at a later time.

However, it's important to note that while humans find comments helpful, the computer doesn't care about them at all. When you run your code, the computer focuses only on the actual code instructions and ignores the comments completely. This separation between code and comments allows you to write code that's both understandable for humans and executable by computers.

So, comments are like your way of adding helpful explanations to your code, ensuring that even if someone else reads it or you revisit it after a while, you'll still understand what's happening and why.

1.5.2 Python Syntax

In Python, the way you space things at the start of a line is super important. Most languages use spacing just to make code look nice, but Python takes it up a notch.

In Python, the spaces you put at the start of a line actually mean something. They show which parts of the code belong together. So, when you put a bunch of lines with the same amount of space at the start, Python knows they're like a team working together. This makes your code organized and easy to read. Other languages use special symbols to do this job, but Python uses spaces to keep things neat and tidy.

Example 1:

```
if 8 > 1:
  print("Eight is greater than one!")
```

Output:

Eight is greater than one!

Example 2:

```
if 8 > 1:
print("Eight is greater than one!")
```

Output:

IndentationError: expected an indented block

1.6 Python framework

Python frameworks are pre-built collections of code and tools that help developers create web applications, software, and other projects more efficiently. These frameworks provide a structured foundation and guidelines for building applications, which can save a lot of time by handling common tasks and implementing best practices. Here are some popular Python frameworks:

Django: A high-level web framework that encourages rapid development and clean, pragmatic design. It provides a lot of built-in features like authentication, database management, URL routing, and more. Django is commonly used for building robust web applications.

Flask: A lightweight web framework that gives you more flexibility to choose your tools and libraries. It's great for smaller projects and offers the basics without imposing too many constraints on your development style.

FastAPI: A modern, fast, web framework for building APIs with Python 3.7+ based on standard Python type hints. It's known for its speed and automatic generation of API documentation.
Pyramid: A flexible and modular framework that allows you to choose the components you need for your project. It's suitable for both small and large applications.
Bottle: A micro web framework that is minimalistic and easy to use. It's designed for simple applications and prototyping.
CherryPy: Another minimalistic framework that provides tools for building web applications in a more object-oriented manner.
Tornado: A web framework and asynchronous networking library that's particularly good for handling real-time applications like chat rooms or streaming.
Web2py: A full-stack framework that includes an integrated development environment (IDE), making it easier to develop, debug, and deploy web applications.

Summary

Key Features:

Clear and elegant syntax.Dynamically typed: Variable types are determined during runtime.Interpreted language: Code is executed line by line without compilation.Versatile and cross-platform: Runs on various operating systems.Extensive standard library: Pre-built modules for various tasks.

Application Areas:

Web development: Frameworks like Django, Flask.Data analysis: Libraries like Pandas, NumPy, and Matplotlib. Scientific computing: Used in research and simulations. Artificial Intelligence (AI) and Machine Learning (ML): Libraries like TensorFlow, PyTorch. Automation and scripting: Automate repetitive tasks. Game development, IoT, and more.

Community and Ecosystem:

Strong and active community of developers. Abundance of third-party libraries and frameworks. Package management using tools like pip. Open-source nature encourages collaboration and innovation.

Readability and Productivity:

Indentation-based syntax enforces code structure. Reduces complexity and enhances code readability. Promotes efficient collaboration among developers.

Learning and Accessibility:

Beginner-friendly language. Suitable for both novice and experienced programmers. Learning resources: Documentation, tutorials, online courses.

Exercise 1:
Multiple-choice questions (MCQs):
Question 1: What type of programming language is Python?
a) Compiled language
b) Low-level language
c) Interpreted language
d) Assembly language
Question 2: Which of the following statements about Python is true?
a) Python is only used for web development.
b) Python code is always executed line by line.
c) Python is not suitable for scientific computing.
d) Python emphasizes code readability and simplicity.
Question 3: Which of the following is a correct way to declare a variable in Python?
a) newVariable = 42
b) 42 = newVariable
c) variable newVariable = 42
d) variable = newVariable(42)
Question 4: What is the purpose of the "print()" function in Python?
a) To display a message on the console.
b) To create a new variable.
c) To perform mathematical calculations.

d) To define a function.

Question 5: Which of the following data types is used to store a sequence of characters in Python?
a) integer
b) float
c) string
d) boolean

Question 6: What is the result of the following code snippet?

```
x = 5
y = 2
result = x ** y
```

a) 7
b) 25
c) 10
d) 8

Question 7: In Python, which keyword is used to create a conditional statement?
a) loop
b) for
c) while
d) if

Question 8: What is the purpose of a "list" in Python?
a) To store only integers.
b) To perform mathematical operations.
c) To store a collection of items, which can be of different data types.
d) To store a single value.

Answer

1. c 2. d 3. a 4. a 5. c 6. b 7. d 8. c

Exercise 2:

True/False Questions:

Question 1: In Python, variables must be declared with a specific data type.
Question 2: Python uses braces {} to define code blocks within loops and conditional statements.
Question 3: The "elif" keyword is used in Python for defining a block of code that executes only if the preceding if and elif conditions are False.
Question 4: The "for" loop in Python is used exclusively for iterating over numerical ranges.
Question 5: Python is not suitable for handling and manipulating strings.

Answer

1.False 2. False 3. True 4. False 5. False

Exercise 3:

Review questions:

Question 1: What is Python and who is its creator?
Question 2: What are some key features that make Python unique compared to other programming languages?
Question 3: Explain the concept of indentation in Python. Why is it important?
Question 4: Name three commonly used libraries and explain their uses.
Question 5: What is the difference between Python 2 and Python 3?
Question 6: How do you write comments in Python and why are comments useful?
Question 7: What is the significance of the print() function? Provide an example.
Question 8: Describe the basic data types available in Python.
Question 9: How do you create a variable in Python? Give an example.
Question 10: What is the difference between a list and a tuple? Provide examples.
Question 11: Explain how to perform basic arithmetic operations in Python.
Question 12: What is typecasting and how can you use it in Python?
Question 13: Explain the concept of loops in Python, and differentiate between a for loop and a while loop.
Question 14: Describe what a function is in Python and how to define one.
Question 15: What is the purpose of conditional statements like if, elif, and else? Provide an example.

Question 16: How are dictionaries different from lists in Python?
Question 17: What is the None type used for in Python?
Question 18: Describe how to read from and write to files in Python.
Question 19: What is PEP 8 and why is it important for Python developers?
Question 20: How do you import modules in Python and what is the significance of the import statement?

Chapter 2

Setting up Python

Setting up Python on your computer is the first step to unlock its coding capabilities. Python is a versatile and widely-used programming language that caters to various applications.

Setting up Python on your computer is an essential but straightforward task that marks the beginning of your programming journey with this versatile language. The process essentially involves downloading the appropriate installer from the Python official website and running it on your system. The installer is generally self-explanatory and guides you through the necessary steps, including the option to add Python to your system PATH, making it easily accessible from the command line.

After installation, you can confirm that Python was installed correctly by invoking it from the command line, terminal, or PowerShell, depending on your operating system. A successful installation will allow you to check the installed version with a simple command, ensuring that the system recognizes Python as an installed application.

It's also worth mentioning that Python often releases new versions with additional features, optimizations, and security fixes. Therefore, keeping your Python installation updated is advisable to benefit from the latest improvements and patches.

In summary, setting up Python is a simple but crucial step that unlocks a wide range of programming capabilities, from web development to data analysis and beyond. The installation not only provides the core language but also includes various tools and utilities that make coding in Python a more efficient and organized endeavour.

2.1 Note on python version

Many operating systems, including macOS and Linux, come with Python preinstalled. The version of Python that comes with your operating system is called the system Python. The system Python is used by your operating system and is usually out of date. It's essential that you have the most recent version of Python so that you can successfully follow along with the examples in this book.

Installing Python is a straightforward process that allows you to set up the programming language on your computer, enabling you to write and run Python code.

Here's a straightforward guide to get you started:

Begin by heading to the official Python website at www.python.org. Once there, locate the "Downloads" section. You'll need to select the appropriate version of Python based on the operating system you're using – whether it's Windows, macOS, or Linux. It's recommended to opt for the latest stable version for the best experience.

This chapter is split into three sections: Windows, macOS, and Ubuntu Linux. Find the section for your operating system and follow the steps to get set up, then skip ahead to the next chapter.

2.2 Installing Python on Windows

Download Python Installer:

Visit the official Python website at https://www.python.org/downloads/windows/ and download the latest version of Python for Windows. Make sure to download the installer that corresponds to your system architecture (32-bit or 64-bit).

Run the Installer:

Once the installer executable (.exe) is downloaded, double-click on it to run it. You might need administrative privileges to install software on your system.

Customize Installation (Optional):

The installer will give you the option to customize the installation. You can choose to add Python to the PATH, which is recommended as it allows you to run Python from the Command Prompt without specifying the full path. You can also choose the installation location and select optional features.

Install Python:

Click the "Install Now" button to start the installation process. The installer will copy the necessary files and set up Python on your system.

Installation Complete:

Once the installation is complete, you will see a screen indicating that Python has been successfully installed. You can also access the Python documentation, browse the Python website, or disable the path length limit. You can also exit the installer.

Verify Installation:

To verify that Python has been installed correctly, open the Command Prompt and type python --version. This should display the version of Python that you installed.

Using Python:

You can now use Python by running scripts or opening an interactive Python shell (REPL) from the Command Prompt. To open the interactive shell, simply type Python in the Command Prompt and press Enter.
That's it! You have successfully installed Python on your Windows system. You can start writing and running Python scripts or experimenting with the Python interactive shell.

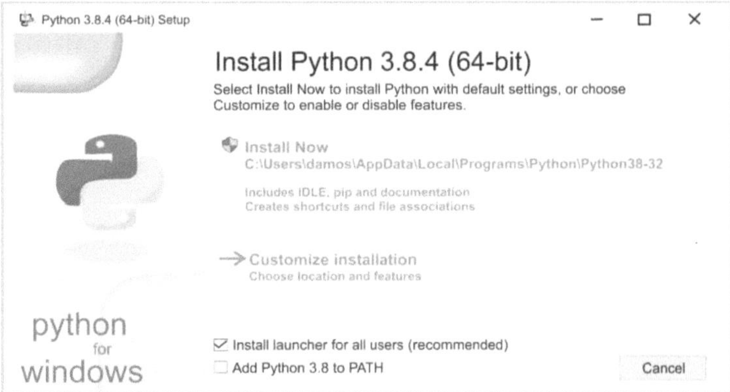

2.3 Install Python on macOS

Check Existing Python Version (Optional):
Open the Terminal and type python --version to check if Python is already installed. macOS typically comes with a pre-installed version of Python 2.x.
Install Homebrew (Optional but Recommended):
Homebrew is a package manager for macOS that makes it easier to install and manage software. To install Homebrew, paste the following command in the Terminal and press Enter:
/bin/bash -c "$(curl -fsSL https://raw.githubusercontent.com/Homebrew/install/HEAD/install.sh)"
Install Python 3:
After installing Homebrew (or if you choose not to use it), you can install Python 3 using the following commands:

- For Homebrew users:
  brew install Python
- Without Homebrew:

Visit the official Python website at https://www.python.org/downloads/macos/ and download the latest version of Python for macOS. Run the installer and follow the prompts.

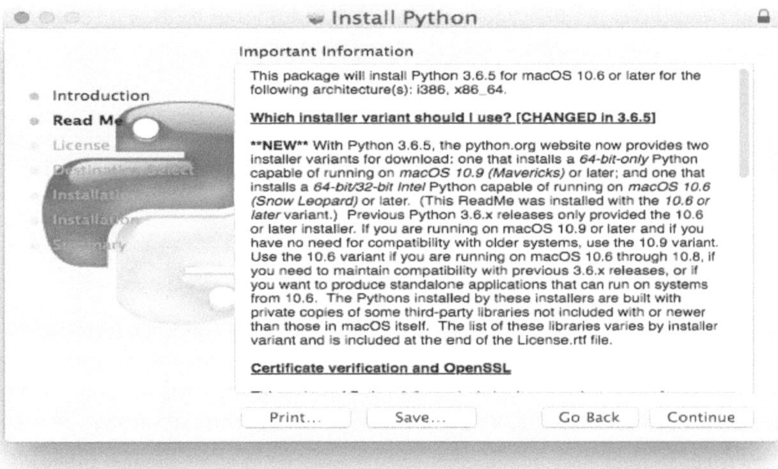

Verify Installation:

After the installation is complete, open a new Terminal window and type python3 --version to verify that Python 3 has been installed. You use python3 to explicitly run Python 3, as macOS typically links the Python command to the pre-installed Python 2.

Using Python:

You can now use Python by running scripts or opening an interactive Python shell in the Terminal. To open the interactive shell, type python3 and press Enter. You can exit the interactive shell by typing exit() or pressing Ctrl + D.

Virtual Environments (Optional but Recommended):

It's a good practice to use virtual environments to manage Python packages for different projects. You can create a virtual environment using the venv module. For example:

```
python3 -m venv myenv
```

Activate the virtual environment:

```
source myenv/bin/activate
```

Deactivate the virtual environment when you're done working:

```
deactivate
```

2.4 Install Python on Ubuntu

To install Python on Ubuntu, you can use the Terminal and follow these steps:

Check Python Version (Optional): Open a terminal by pressing Ctrl + Alt + T and type the following command to check if Python is already installed along with its version:

python3 –version

This command will tell you the version of Python 3 that's installed, which is the recommended version.

Update Package Lists:

Before installing any software, it's a good idea to update the package lists to make sure you're getting the latest versions. In the terminal, run:

sudo apt update

Install Python:

To install Python 3, use the following command:

sudo apt install python3

Verify Installation:

After the installation is complete, you can verify it by running:

python3 –version

This should display the version number of the Python interpreter you just installed.

Install pip (Python Package Manager) (Optional): Pip is a package manager for Python that makes it easy to install and manage additional libraries and packages. You can install it with:

sudo apt install python3-pip

Install Additional Tools (Optional):

Depending on your needs, you might want to install some additional tools. For example, if you're planning to work with virtual environments, you can install the **venv** module:

sudo apt install python3-venv

Now you have Python successfully installed on your Ubuntu system. You can start writing and running Python scripts by opening a terminal and using the **python3** command followed by your script's filename. If you're using an Integrated Development Environment (IDE) like Visual Studio Code, you can use it to create and run Python code as well.

Summary

Windows Installation: Installing Windows involves booting from a Windows installation media (such as a USB drive or DVD) and following on-screen prompts. Users can choose custom settings, partition their storage, and select the version of Windows they want to install. The process includes entering a product key, configuring language and region settings, and creating a user account. Windows provides a step-by-step setup wizard, making it relatively straightforward for users.

macOS Installation: Installing macOS typically requires an Apple computer. Users can download the latest macOS version from the Mac App Store. The installation process involves running the installer, which guides users through setting up the language, keyboard layout, and other preferences. macOS installation often includes migrating data from a previous installation or a Time Machine backup. Apple's guided interface simplifies the process for users familiar with Apple's ecosystem.

Ubuntu Installation: Ubuntu installation starts with downloading an ISO image from the official website. Users can create a bootable USB drive using tools like Rufus or BalenaEtcher. To install Ubuntu, users boot from the USB drive and choose between trying Ubuntu or installing it. The installer guides users through language, keyboard, and network settings, partitioning the disk, and creating a user account. Users can also decide whether to install third-party software and updates during installation.

Each operating system installation process varies in terms of complexity, requirements, and available options. While Windows offers a guided installation with customization choices, macOS focuses on an Apple-centric experience, and Ubuntu emphasizes user control and open-source flexibility.

Exercise 1:

Multiple-choice questions (MCQs):

Question 1: Which of the following is NOT a way to install Python on your system?
a) Downloading it from the official Python website.
b) Using a package manager like pip.
c) Installing it through a web browser.
d) Using an integrated development environment (IDE).

Question 2: Which command is commonly used in the terminal to check if Python is installed?
a) python check
b) python -v
c) python version
d) python --version

Question 3: What is a virtual environment in Python used for?
A) Running Python code in a separate virtual reality environment.
b) Isolating Python projects to manage dependencies separately.
c) Running Python code on cloud servers.
d) Creating a separate Python interpreter for each program.

Question 4: Which tool is used to manage Python packages and dependencies?
a) VENV
b) ENV
c) PIP
d) PYENV

Question 5: Which file is commonly used to specify project dependencies and their versions?
a) requirements.txt
b) dependencies.py
c) package.json
d) depend.yml

Question 6: Which command is used to create a virtual environment using VENV?
a) venv create myenv
b) python -m venv myenv
c) venv myenv
d) python create venv myenv

Question 7: An integrated development environment (IDE) for Python provides:
a) Only basic text editing features.
b) A code editor, debugger, and other helpful tools.
c) Only a terminal interface.
d) Support for a single Python version.

Question 8: Which Python version should you choose if you want the latest features and improvements?
a) Python 2.7
b) Python 3.0
c) The latest Python 3.x version (e.g., Python 3.9)
d) Python 4.0

Answer

1. c 2. d 3. b 4. c 5. a 6. b 7.b 8.c

Exercise 2:

True/False Questions:

Question 1: Python can be installed on Windows, but it's not compatible with macOS.
Question 2: Setting up a virtual environment is recommended to isolate dependencies for different projects.
Question 3: PIP is a package manager used for installing Python packages, but it doesn't manage virtual environments.
Question 4: Python 2.x and Python 3.x can be installed side by side on the same system without any conflicts.
Question 5: An IDE provides tools that make coding in Python easier, but it's not necessary for setting up and running Python code.

Answer

1. False 2. True 3. False 4. True 5. True

Exercise 3:

Review questions:

Question 1: What are the basic system requirements for installing Python?
Question 2: What is the latest stable version of Python as of your last update?
Question 3: Describe the difference between Python 2.x and Python 3.x.
Question 4: How do you download the Python installer for Windows?
Question 5: What are the steps to install Python on a macOS system?
Question 6: What is the PATH variable and why is it important when setting up Python?
Question 7: What is the role of the Python Software Foundation in the development and distribution of Python?
Question 8: How do you verify that Python was successfully installed on your system?
Question 9: What is a Python IDE, and can you name a few popular ones?
Question 10: What is a virtual environment and why might you want to use one?
Question 11: How do you upgrade Python to a newer version on your system?
Question 12: What is Anaconda, and how does it relate to setting up Python for data science?
Question 13: How can you install Python packages using **pip**?
Question 14: What is the significance of the **site-packages** directory in a Python installation?
Question 15: What is Jupyter Notebook, and how do you set it up after installing Python?
Question 16: Can Python co-exist with other programming languages on the same computer?
Question 17: How do you set up Python on a Linux system?
Question 18: What are some common issues people face when installing Python, and how can they be resolved?
Question 19: What are environment variables in the context of a Python setup?
Question 20: How do you uninstall Python from your system, and what are the considerations to keep in mind when doing so?

Chapter 3

Variables in Python

In the world of programming, variables are like containers that hold different types of information. They enable you to store and manage data within your Python programs. Think of variables as labelled boxes that you can use to keep track of values, making your code dynamic and flexible.

variables act as placeholders or containers for storing data values. Unlike languages that require a strict definition of data types upon variable declaration, Python employs dynamic typing, allowing variables to change types during runtime. This lends Python both flexibility and user-friendliness, making it easier for beginners to pick up the language while still providing the robustness needed for advanced programming.

Naming Conventions and Rules: Variable names must adhere to a set of rules and conventions. They should begin with a letter or an underscore and can be followed by letters, numbers, or underscores. Python is case-sensitive, meaning Variable and variable would be two distinct variables. Reserved keywords like for, while, and if cannot be used as variable names. Following PEP 8 guidelines for variable naming—using lowercase with underscores for multi-word names—is generally considered best practice.

Dynamic Typing: One of the most distinctive features of Python variables is dynamic typing. The interpreter automatically identifies the data type of a variable based on the value it holds. This means that a variable can change its type during the execution of the program.

Immutable vs Mutable Data Types: Variables in Python can hold either mutable or immutable data types. Immutable types include integers, floats, strings, and tuples. Once an immutable variable is set, its contents cannot be altered, although the variable can be reassigned. Mutable types, such as lists and dictionaries, allow for the modification of their elements.

Variable Scope: The scope of a variable refers to the region of the code where the variable can be accessed or modified. Python supports global, local, and non-local (in the case of nested functions) variable scopes. Local variables are confined to the function in which they are defined, whereas global variables are accessible throughout the module. The global and nonlocal keywords can be used to alter the scope of a variable.

Type Inference: Python employs type inference to determine the data type of a variable. When a variable is assigned a particular value, Python automatically sets its type. This alleviates the need for explicit type declaration, although the type can be explicitly checked using the type() function.

Memory Management: Python's memory management for variables is abstracted, meaning that the programmer doesn't have to explicitly allocate or deallocate memory for variables. The Python memory manager takes care of this internally. When a variable is no longer in use, Python's garbage collector automatically frees the memory.

Variables in Python serve as an essential building block, providing a flexible and dynamic way to store, manipulate, and pass data throughout a program. Their features and capabilities make them one of the key elements contributing to Python's simplicity and power.

3.1 Variables

1. Assigning Values: To create a variable, you assign a value to it using the equals sign (=). For instance:

```
name = "Alice"
age = 30
```

2. Variable Names: Variable names are used to identify and access the data stored within them. Names must follow specific rules:

- Start with a letter or underscore (_), followed by letters, digits, or underscores.
- Avoid using reserved words (like **if**, **for**, **while**, etc.).
- Variable names are case-sensitive, so **name** and **Name** are different variables.

3. Data Types: Python is dynamically typed, meaning variables can change data types. For example, you can switch from storing an integer to a string in the same variable:

```
age = 30
age = "thirty"
```

4. Types of Data: Variables can hold various types of data, including:

- **Numbers:** Integers (**int**) and floating-point numbers (**float**).
- **Text:** Strings (**str**) for sequences of characters.
- **Boolean: True** or **False** values (**bool**).
- **Collections:** Lists, tuples, and dictionaries to store multiple values.

5. Using Variables: You can perform operations using variables just like you would with the actual values:

```
x = 10
```

y = 5
sum = x + y

6. Reassignment: Variables can be reassigned with new values:

name = "Bob"
name = "Charlie"

7. Readability and Clarity: Choose meaningful variable names that reflect the purpose of the data they hold. This enhances the readability of your code for you and others.

8. Variable Scope: Variables have a scope, which defines where they can be accessed. Variables created inside a function are local to that function, while those defined outside are usually considered global.

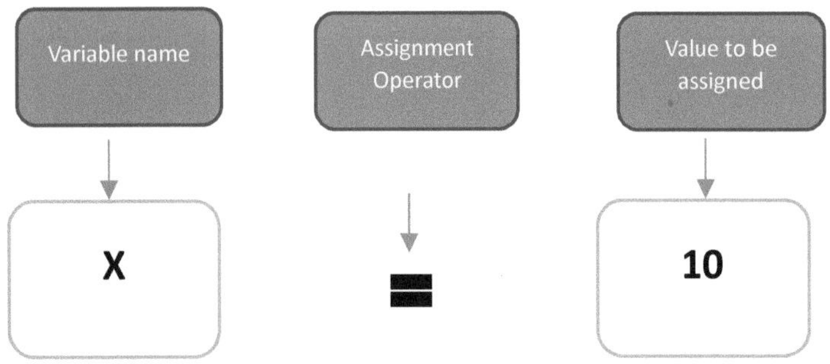

3.1.1 Creating variables in Python:

Creating variables in Python is simple. You can create a variable by giving it a name and assigning a value to it using the equal sign (=) operator. Here's how you can do it:

```
# Assigning a string value to a variable named 'name'
name = "Alice"
# Assigning an integer value to a variable named 'age'
age = 30
# Assigning a floating-point value to a variable named 'salary'
salary = 50000.0
# Assigning a boolean value to a variable named 'is_student'
is_student = True
```

In the code above:

- **name** is a variable that holds a string value ("Alice").
- **age** is a variable that holds an integer value (30).
- **salary** is a variable that holds a floating-point value (50000.0).
- **is_student** is a variable that holds a boolean value (**True**).

You can also change the value of a variable by reassigning it:

```
name = "Joy"  # Changing the value of the 'name' variable
age = 46     # Changing the value of the 'age' variable
```

Remember, variable names should follow certain rules:

- Start with a letter (a-z or A-Z) or an underscore (_).
- Subsequent characters can be letters, digits (0-9), or underscores.
- Variable names are case-sensitive, so **name** and **Name** would be considered different variables.

Choosing meaningful and descriptive variable names helps improve the readability and maintainability of your code.

3.1.2 Casting Variable in Python:

Casting a variable in Python refers to the process of changing the data type of a variable from one type to another. Sometimes, you might need to convert a variable from one data type to another to perform certain operations or achieve specific functionality. Python provides various built-in functions that allow you to perform these type conversions. Here are some common type casting functions in Python:

int(): This function is used to convert a value to an integer data type.

```
float_number = 3.14
int_number = int(float_number)  # Converts the float to an integer
```

float(): This function is used to convert a value to a floating-point data type.

```
int_number = 42
```

float_number = float(int_number) # Converts the integer to a float
str(): This function is used to convert a value to a string data type.
number = 123
text = str(number) # Converts the number to a string
bool(): This function is used to convert a value to a boolean data type.
number = 0
boolean_value = bool(number) # Converts the number to a boolean (False)
list(), tuple(), dict(): These functions are used to convert values to list, tuple, and dictionary data types, respectively.
text = "hello"
list_version = list(text) # Converts the string to a list of characters ['h', 'e', 'l', 'l', 'o']

Casting variables is important when you want to perform operations that are only valid for specific data types. Keep in mind that not all type conversions are possible or make sense. For instance, you can't always convert a string containing letters to an integer if the string isn't a valid number.

It's a good practice to use type casting with caution and ensure that the conversion is meaningful and accurate for your specific use case.

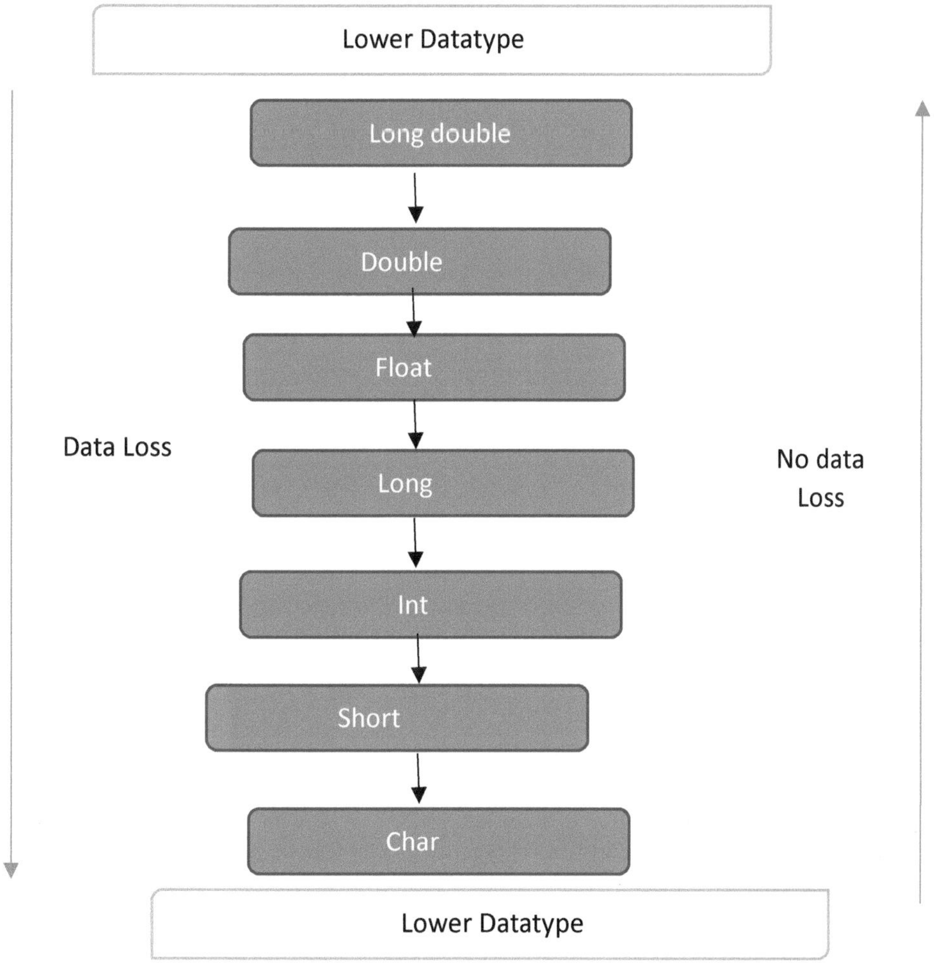

3.1.3 Get the type in Python?

In Python, every value and variable has a specific data type associated with it. The data type defines what kind of value it represents, such as a number, a piece of text, or a collection of values. Sometimes, you might need to know the data type of a variable to make sure you're working with it correctly, especially when dealing with complex code or performing certain operations.

The type() function is a built-in function in Python that allows you to find out the data type of a variable or a value. Here's how it works:

```
x = 5
print(type(x))  # Outputs: <class 'int'>

y = "hello"
print(type(y))  # Outputs: <class 'str'>

z = [1, 2, 3]
print(type(z))  # Outputs: <class 'list'>
```

In the examples above, the **type()** function is used to determine the data types of variables **x**, **y**, and **z**. When you run the code, it prints out the class type associated with each variable.

- **type(x)** returns **<class 'int'>**, indicating that **x** is of the integer data type.
- **type(y)** returns **<class 'str'>**, indicating that **y** is of the string data type.
- **type(z)** returns **<class 'list'>**, indicating that **z** is of the list data type.

You can see that the **type()** function returns the class type enclosed in single quotes (**' '**), which gives you information about the data type.

Using the **type()** function is particularly useful when you're working with complex code that involves multiple data types, or when you need to ensure that a variable has the expected data type before performing certain operations. It's a handy tool for maintaining control and understanding the behaviour of your code as you work with different types of data.

Dynamic Typing in Python:

Python is a dynamically typed language, which means that you don't need to explicitly declare the data type of a variable when you create it. The interpreter automatically determines the data type based on the value assigned to the variable. This flexibility allows you to easily change the value and type of a variable during program execution.

Using type() for Decision-Making:

The ability to determine the data type of a variable is crucial when making decisions in your code. For example, you might want to perform different actions based on the data type:

```
value = input("Enter something: ")

if type(value) == int:
   print("You entered an integer.")
elif type(value) == str:
   print("You entered a string.")
else:
   print("You entered something else.")
```

Type Checking and Validation:

Type checking becomes important when dealing with user inputs or external data sources. You can use the type() function to validate whether the input matches the expected data type before processing it:

```
user_input = input("Enter an integer: ")

if user_input.isdigit():
   integer_value = int(user_input)
   print("You entered:", integer_value)
else:
   print("Invalid input. Please enter an integer.")
```

Avoiding Unexpected Behavior:

Understanding the data type of variables helps you avoid unexpected behavior that can arise from combining incompatible types. For instance, adding a number and a string might lead to errors if you're not aware of the types involved.

```
number = 5
text = "10"
result = number + text  # This would raise an error due to mixing types
```

By using the **type()** function, you can better anticipate such scenarios and handle them appropriately in your code.

3.2 Python - Variable Names

In programming, naming conventions for variables help improve readability and maintainability of the code. Variable names are not just placeholders for values; they serve as clues to understanding what the code does. Below elaborate on the naming conventions you mentioned.

Variable Names

A variable can have a short name (like x and y) or a more descriptive name (age, carname, total_volume). Rules for Python variables:

- A variable name must start with a letter or the underscore character
- A variable name cannot start with a number
- A variable name can only contain alpha-numeric characters and underscores (A-z, 0-9, and _)
- Variable names are case-sensitive (age, Age and AGE are three different variables)
- A variable name cannot be any of the Python keywords.

Example:

Legal variable names:

```
myvar = "John"
my_var = "John"
_my_var = "John"
myVar = "John"
MYVAR = "John"
myvar2 = "John"
```

1. Camel Case

In camel case, the first letter of the variable name starts in lowercase, and the first letter of each subsequent concatenated word starts with an uppercase letter. There are no spaces or underscores between words.

Example:

```
myVariableName = "John"
```

The first word "my" is all in lowercase.

The first letter of each of the subsequent words ("Variable", "Name") is capitalized.

Use case: Camel case is widely used in languages like Java and JavaScript. It's also fairly common in Python, especially for naming functions and variables.

2. Pascal Case

Pascal case is similar to camel case, but the first letter of the first word is also capitalized. This is why it's sometimes called "Upper Camel Case."

Example:

```
MyVariableName = "John"
```

The first letter of each word ("My", "Variable", "Name") is capitalized.

Use case: Pascal case is often used in languages like C# to name classes. In Python, it's conventional to name classes using Pascal case.

3. Snake Case

In snake case, words are separated by underscores and all letters are lowercase. Snake case is more readable when variable names have multiple words.

Example:

```
my_variable_name = "John"
```

- All words ("my", "variable", "name") are in lowercase.
- Words are separated by underscores.

Use case: Snake case is the most common naming convention for variables and functions in Python, especially when the name consists of multiple words that make up a descriptive identifier.

3.3 Python Variables - Assign Multiple Values

In Python, you can assign multiple values to multiple variables in a single line. This can make your code more concise and potentially more readable. Here are some ways to do it:

1. Basic Multiple Assignment

You can assign values to multiple variables in one line, separating variables and values by commas.

```
a, b, c = 1, 2, 3
```

In this example, **a** will be 1, **b** will be 2, and **c** will be 3.

2. Assign the Same Value to Multiple Variables

You can also assign a single value to multiple variables simultaneously.

```
a = b = c = 1
```

Here, **a**, **b**, and **c** will all have the value 1.

3. Unpacking Lists or Tuples

You can unpack a list or tuple, assigning its elements to individual variables.

```
my_list = [1, 2, 3]
a, b, c = my_list
```

After this operation, **a** will be 1, **b** will be 2, and **c** will be 3.

4. Using the Asterisk (*) for Extended Unpacking

If the number of variables is less than the number of elements in the list or tuple, you can use the * symbol to collect remaining elements into a list.

```
a, *b = [1, 2, 3, 4]
```

Here, **a** will be 1, and **b** will be **[2, 3, 4]**.

5. Unpacking Nested Lists or Tuples

You can even unpack nested lists or tuples.

```
a, (b, c), d = [1, (2, 3), 4]
```

After this, a will be 1, b will be 2, c will be 3, and d will be 4.

6. Swapping Variables

Multiple assignments can be used for swapping two variables without requiring a temporary variable.

If a was 1 and b was 2, after this operation a will be 2 and b will be 1.

7. Dictionary Unpacking

You can also use multiple assignments with dictionaries, although this is less common and may make the code less readable.

Here, **a**, **b**, and **c** will get the values 1, 2, and 3, respectively. Note that this depends on the dictionary maintaining insertion order, a feature guaranteed as of Python 3.7.

Important Points

Make sure the number of variables matches the number of values, or Python will throw an error. The exception to this rule is when you're using extended unpacking with the asterisk *.

The unpacking sequence should be inerrable; otherwise, Python will throw an error.

While these features can make your code more concise, they can also make it less readable if overused or used in complex ways. Always prioritize readability over brevity.

3.4 Type of Variable in Python

In Python, variables can be classified as either global or local based on their scope, which is essentially the portion of the code where the variable can be accessed or modified. Understanding these scopes is crucial for effective programming and avoiding bugs.

Global Variables

A global variable is a variable that is declared outside of any function or is explicitly marked as global within a function. It can be accessed and modified from anywhere in the code after its declaration, both inside and outside of functions, provided that the variable is in scope.

Example of Global Variable:

```
x = 10  # This is a global variable

def my_function():
   print("Value of x inside function:", x)

my_function()
print("Value of x outside function:", x)
```

Output:

```
Value of x inside function: 10
Value of x outside function: 10
```

To modify a global variable from within a function, you have to explicitly state that you want to use the global version of the variable using the **global** keyword:

```
x = 10  # This is a global variable

def modify_global():
   global x
   x = 20  # Modifying the global variable

modify_global()
print("Modified global x:", x)  # Output: Modified global x: 20
```

Local Variables

A local variable is a variable declared inside a function. It can only be accessed and modified within that function, making it isolated from the rest of the code.

Example of Local Variable:

```
def my_function():
    y = 20  # This is a local variable
    print("Value of y inside function:", y)

my_function()
# Uncommenting the line below will raise an error
# print("Value of y outside function:", y)  # Error, y is not defined
```

Interaction Between Global and Local Variables

You can have local and global variables with the same name. In such cases, the local variable inside the function will take precedence over the global variable.

Example:

```
x = 10  # Global variable

def my_function():
    x = 5  # Local variable
    print("Local x:", x)

my_function()
print("Global x:", x)
```

Output:

```
Local x: 5
Global x: 10
```

In the above example, **x = 5** inside **my_function** does not affect the global **x**.

Key Points to Remember:

Shadowing: When a local variable has the same name as a global variable, it shadows the global variable within that function. This can sometimes lead to bugs.

Best Practices: It's generally considered better practice to avoid using global variables when possible, as they can make the program harder to understand and debug.

Global Keyword: The global keyword allows you to specify that a variable inside a function refers to a global variable.

Nonlocal Keyword: For nested functions, Python also provides the nonlocal keyword to work with variables in the nearest enclosing scope that is not global.

Immutability: If a global variable refers to an immutable type (like a string or tuple), you have to use the global keyword to modify it. However, if it refers to a mutable type (like a list or dictionary), you can modify its contents without the global keyword.

Understanding the scope of variables is critical for effective Python programming. Local variables help to encapsulate and localize variables to where they are used, making the program easier to manage, while global variables are useful for sharing data between different parts of a program.

3.5 Delete variable in Python

In Python, you can delete a variable using the **del** keyword. The **del** keyword removes the variable's reference to the value it was holding, effectively deleting the variable. After a variable has been deleted, attempting to reference it will result in a **NameError** since the variable no longer exists in the scope.

Here are some examples:

Deleting a Simple Variable

```
x = 10
print(x)  # Output will be 10

del x  # Delete the variable x

# Trying to print x now will raise a NameError
# print(x)  # Uncommenting this line will raise: NameError: name 'x' is not defined
```

Deleting an Element from a List or Dictionary

You can also use **del** to remove items from a list or keys from a dictionary.

For a list:

```
my_dict = {'a': 1, 'b': 2, 'c': 3}
del my_dict['b']  # Remove the key-value pair with key 'b'
print(my_dict)  # Output will be {'a': 1, 'c': 3}
```

Deleting Multiple Variables

You can delete multiple variables at once by separating them with commas.

```
x = 10
y = 20
z = 30

del x, y, z
# All three variables (x, y, z) are now deleted
```

Note:

Using **del** on a variable removes the reference, but it doesn't necessarily "free" the memory immediately. Python's garbage collector will take care of reclaiming the unused memory.

Deleting a variable that doesn't exist will raise a **NameError**.

Deleting an object variable does not remove the object itself if there are other references to the object. It merely removes that one reference.

By understanding how and when to use **del**, you can manage your variables more effectively.

Summary

In Python, variables are used to store and manage data in a program. They are dynamically typed, meaning their type is determined at runtime based on the value they hold. Common data types include integers, floats, strings, lists, dictionaries, and many more. Variables must adhere to certain naming conventions, such as starting with a letter or an underscore but not with a number. They can only contain alpha-numeric characters and are case-sensitive.

Variables in Python have different scopes; they can be global, local, or within specific namespaces like classes and functions. Global variables are accessible throughout the entire code, while local variables are confined to the function or block in which they are declared. The **global** and **nonlocal** keywords allow you to manipulate the scope of a variable within a function.

In terms of naming conventions, Python allows various styles including Camel Case (**myVariable**), Pascal Case (**MyVariable**), and Snake Case (**my_variable**). The choice of style often depends on the coding guidelines being followed.

Python also provides mechanisms for advanced variable operations. For instance, multiple variables can be assigned in a single line (**a, b = 1, 2**), and variables can even be unpacked from complex data structures. Variables can be deleted from the program using the **del** keyword, which removes their reference, leaving the task of reclaiming unused memory to Python's garbage collector.

Overall, understanding variables in Python is fundamental to effective programming, as they are the building blocks for storing and manipulating data.

Exercise 1:

Multiple Choice Questions (MCQs):

Question 1: Which of the following is a valid variable name in Python?

a) 1variable

b) variable_name

c) variable-name

d) variable name

Question 2: Which of the following data type does not exist in Python?

a) str

b) float

c) char

d) bool

Question 3: Which of the following is used to unpack multiple values into variables?

a) ()

b) []

c) {}

d) ,
Question 4: Which keyword is used to refer to a global variable inside a function?
a) local
b) global
c) extern
d) public
Question 5: Which of the following styles is known as "Camel Case"?
a) myVariableName
b) my_variable_name
c) MyVariableName
d) MYVARIABLENAME
Question 6: Which keyword allows you to manipulate a variable from an outer (but non-global) scope?
a) global
b) nonlocal
c) external
d) outer
Question 7: Which of the following will raise an error in Python?
a) x, y = 1, 2
b) x y = 3 4
c) x = y = 5
d) x, = [1]
Question 8: After which command will the variable **x** be completely deleted?
a) remove(x)
b) pop(x)
c) erase(x)
d) del x
Answers
1. b 2. c 3. d 4. b 5.a 6. 7.b 8.b 9.d

Exercise 2:
True/False Questions:
Question 1: In Python, variable names can start with a number.
Question 2: Python is a statically typed language.
Question 3: The variable names **myVariable**, **myvariable**, and **MYVARIABLE** are all the same in Python.
Question 4: We can delete items from a list or dictionary using the **del** keyword.
Question 5: A variable declared inside a function in Python is always considered global.
Answer
1. False 2. False 3. False 4. True 5. False

Exercise 3:
Review questions:
Question 1: What is a variable in Python, and what role does it play in programming?
Question 2: How do you declare a variable in Python?
Question 3: What are the naming conventions for variables in Python?
Question 4: Can a variable name start with a number? Why or why not?
Question 5: How do you assign multiple variables in a single line?
Question 6: How do you assign the same value to multiple variables simultaneously?
Question 7: What is the difference between local and global variables?
Question 8: How do you convert a string variable to an integer?
Question 9: What happens when you try to use a variable before assigning a value to it?
Question 10: What is variable unpacking, and how is it done with lists or tuples?
Question 11: What does the id() function reveal about a variable?
Question 12: How do you check the data type of a variable?
Question 13: What is type casting, and how can it be applied to variables?
Question 14: Can variables in Python hold more than one type of data? Explain.

Question 15: What does it mean for variables to be "strongly typed" in Python?
Question 16: How are variables passed in functions: by reference or by value?
Question 17: What are mutable and immutable types in the context of variable assignment?
Question 18: How do you swap the values of two variables without using a third variable?
Question 19: What is the scope of a variable, and how does it affect the variable's accessibility in different parts of a program?
Question 20: What is the difference between the = and == operators with respect to variables?

Chapter 4

String in Python

Strings in Python are sequences of characters, which can include letters, numbers, symbols, and spaces. They are used to represent and manipulate text-based data. In Python, strings are enclosed within either single (' ') or double (" ") quotation marks. Here are a few examples of strings:
"Hello, world!"
'Python is fun!'
"12345"
"Special characters: !@#$%^&*"
Strings are considered immutable, meaning that once created, their contents cannot be changed. However, you can create new strings by manipulating existing ones. Strings can be combined (concatenated), split, sliced, and modified using various string methods and operations provided by Python. They are fundamental for working with textual information and are extensively used in programming for tasks like input/output, formatting, and text processing. In Python, strings are more than just a sequence of characters. They come packed with a variety of features and functions that make text manipulation easy. While you can't change a string after it's been created due to its immutability, you can always create new strings by altering the existing ones. This is possible through various string methods Python offers, like converting the case of the text, replacing substrings, or trimming white spaces.
Strings in Python are objects, offering a broad range of built-in methods for operations like searching, splitting, and formatting. This makes it convenient to perform complex string manipulations without needing additional libraries. Another powerful feature is string interpolation, which allows for the embedding of variables within a string. This can be particularly useful for generating dynamic messages or output.
Beyond the basics, Python's string handling capabilities extend to more advanced features such as Unicode support. This is crucial for applications that require multi-language text processing. Additionally, Python provides special escape characters for incorporating non-printable characters into your strings, such as newlines or tabs. If you need to include such special characters as part of your string, you can use Python's raw strings, which treat backslashes as literal characters.
For situations where a string spans multiple lines, Python provides triple quotes, which are also commonly used for writing docstrings. This feature helps you write more readable code and documentation without worrying about escape characters for line breaks.
Python's string handling abilities go far beyond merely storing sequences of characters. They offer a host of powerful features that provide extensive flexibility and functionality for text manipulation tasks.

4.1 What are strings in Python?

Creating strings in Python can be done by enclosing characters within either single or double quotes. Python also offers triple quotes, which are primarily used for multiline strings or docstrings.

Using single quotes:

```
string1 = 'Hello Python'
print(string1)
```

Using double quotes:

```
string2 = "Hello Python"
print(string2)
```

Using triple quotes:

```
string3 = """Triple quotes are often employed to
   represent multiline content or
   docstrings'''
print(string3)
```

Rephrased: You can make strings in Python by putting characters inside single or double quotes. There's also the option of using triple quotes, mainly for creating text that spans multiple lines or for docstrings.
For instance:

Using single quotes:

```
text1 = 'Hello Python'
print(text1)
```

Using double quotes:

```
text2 = "Hello Python"
print(text2)
```

Using triple quotes:

```
text3 = """Triple quotes are commonly used to
   show content that goes over multiple lines or
   for docstrings"'
print(text3)
```

4.2. String slicing

Strings in Python are sequences of characters, which can include letters, numbers, symbols, and spaces. They are used to represent and manipulate text-based data. In Python, strings are enclosed within either single (' ') or double (" ") quotation marks. Here are a few examples of strings:

"Hello, world!"
'Python is fun!'
"12345"
"Special characters: !@#$%^&*"

Strings are considered immutable, meaning that once created, their contents cannot be changed. However, you can create new strings by manipulating existing ones. Strings can be combined (concatenated), split, sliced, and modified using various string methods and operations provided by Python. They are fundamental for working with textual information and are extensively used in programming for tasks like input/output, formatting, and text processing.

Syntax:

string[start:end:step]

start: The index of the first character you want to include in the slice. This character will be included in the output.

end: The index of the first character you want to exclude from the slice. This character will not be included in the output.

step: An optional parameter that determines the step size or how many characters to skip between each character in the slice.

It's important to note that:

The character at the **start** index is included in the slice.

The character at the **end** index is not included in the slice.

If **start** is omitted, it defaults to 0 (the beginning of the string).

If **end** is omitted, it defaults to the end of the string.

If **step** is omitted, it defaults to 1 (every character in the range).

Here are some examples to illustrate string slicing:

```
text = "Python is amazing"
# Extract characters from index 7 to 9 (inclusive start, exclusive end)
print(text[7:10])  # Output: "is"

# Extract characters from index 0 to 5
print(text[:6])    # Output: "Python"

# Extract characters from index 10 to the end
print(text[10:])   # Output: "amazing"

# Extract every second character from the whole string
print(text[::2])   # Output: "Pto saaig"

# Reverse the string using a negative step
print(text[::-1])  # Output: "gnizama si nohtyP"
```

String slicing is a powerful tool for extracting specific parts of strings without modifying the original string. It's commonly used for tasks like data extraction, text manipulation, and formatting. Just remember that the indices used for slicing are zero-based, meaning the first character is at index 0, the second character is at index 1, and so on

4.3 String Modifying

1. Changing Case: Python provides methods to change the case of strings:

upper(): Converts the entire string to uppercase.

lower(): Converts the entire string to lowercase.

capitalize(): Capitalizes the first character and makes the rest lowercase.

title(): Capitalizes the first character of each word in the string.

Example:
text = "Hello World"
upper_text = text.upper() # "HELLO WORLD"
lower_text = text.lower() # "hello world"
capital_text = text.capitalize() # "Hello world"
title_text = text.title() # "Hello World"

2. Removing Whitespaces: Python provides methods to remove whitespace characters from strings:
strip(): Removes leading and trailing spaces.
lstrip(): Removes leading spaces.
rstrip(): Removes trailing spaces.

Example:
text = "   Some text with spaces   "
stripped_text = text.strip() # "Some text with spaces"
left_stripped = text.lstrip() # "Some text with spaces   "
right_stripped = text.rstrip() # "   Some text with spaces"

3. Replacing Substrings: You can replace specific substrings within a string using the **replace()** method:
Example:
text = "I like apples and oranges"
new_text = text.replace("apples", "bananas") # "I like bananas and oranges"

4. Splitting Strings: The **split()** method divides a string into substrings based on a specified delimiter (default is space). It returns a list of substrings.
Example:
text = "apple,banana,orange"
fruits = text.split(",") # ['apple', 'banana', 'orange']

5. Joining Strings: You can join a list of strings into a single string using the **join()** method:
Example:
fruits = ['apple', 'banana', 'orange']
combined = ", ".join(fruits) # "apple, banana, orange"

4.4 String Method

len(): Returns the length (number of characters) of a string.
Example:
text = "Hello"
length = len(text) # 5

str.upper() and str.lower(): Converts the string to uppercase or lowercase.
Example:
text = "Hello World"
upper_text = text.upper() # "HELLO WORLD"
lower_text = text.lower() # "hello world"

str.capitalize() and str.title(): Capitalizes the first character or each word in the string.
Example:
text = "hello world"
capital_text = text.capitalize() # "Hello world"
title_text = text.title() # "Hello World"

str.strip(), str.lstrip(), and str.rstrip(): Removes leading/trailing spaces or specific characters.
Example:
ext = "   Spaces   "
stripped_text = text.strip() # "Spaces"
left_stripped = text.lstrip() # "Spaces   "
right_stripped = text.rstrip() # "   Spaces"

str.replace(old, new): Replaces occurrences of a substring with another substring.
Example:
text = "I like apples"

new_text = text.replace("apples", "bananas") # "I like bananas"

str.split(delimiter): Splits the string into a list of substrings based on a delimiter.
Example:
text = "apple,banana,orange"
fruits = text.split(",") # ['apple', 'banana', 'orange']

str.join(iterable): Joins elements of an iterable into a string using the specified string as a separator.
Example:
fruits = ['apple', 'banana', 'orange']
combined = ", ".join(fruits) # "apple, banana, orange"

str.find(substring) and str.rfind(substring): Searches for the first/last occurrence of a substring and returns its index. If not found, returns -1.
Example:
text = "Hello, World!"
index = text.find("World") # 7
r_index = text.rfind("l") # 10 (last 'l')

str.startswith(prefix) and str.endswith(suffix): Checks if the string starts or ends with a specific prefix or suffix.
Example:
text = "Hello, World!"
starts_with = text.startswith("Hello") # True
ends_with = text.endswith("!") # True

str.count(substring): Counts the number of occurrences of a substring in the string.
Example:
text = "hello, hello world"
count = text.count("hello") # 2

str.isalpha(), str.isdigit(), str.isalnum(), str.isspace(): Check if the string consists of alphabetic characters, digits, alphanumeric characters, or whitespace characters, respectively.
Example:
alpha_check = "Hello".isalpha() # True
digit_check = "12345".isdigit() # True
alnum_check = "Hello123".isalnum() # True
space_check = "   ".isspace() # True
These are just some of the many string methods available in Python. By combining these methods, you can effectively manipulate, transform, and analyze string data to meet your programming needs.

4.5. Concatinate String

String concatenation in Python refers to the process of combining multiple strings together to create a single string. This is achieved using the + operator or other string manipulation techniques. Concatenation allows you to merge the contents of different strings into one continuous string.
For example:
first_name = "John"
last_name = "Doe"
full_name = first_name + " " + last_name
print(full_name) # Output: "John Doe"
In this example, the + operator is used to concatenate the **first_name**, a space, and the **last_name** to create the **full_name** string.
For instance, if you have two strings, **a** and **b**, you can merge them by adding them together:
a = "Hello"
b = "World"
c = a + b
print(c)
This would result in **c** containing the concatenated string "HelloWorld".

If you want to include a space between the concatenated strings, you can add a space within quotation marks:

```
a = "Hello"
b = "World"
c = a + " " + b
print(c)
```

Here, **c** will hold the string "Hello World".

String concatenation is commonly used when you need to create meaningful sentences, messages, or labels by combining various pieces of text dynamically. It's a fundamental operation when working with text data and allows you to build more complex strings from simpler ones.

String concatenation in Python involves using the + operator to combine strings. You can add additional characters like spaces or symbols between the strings as needed.

4.6. String Formatting:

String formatting in Python refers to the process of creating strings that include placeholders to represent variables or values, and then filling in those placeholders with actual values. This makes it easier to construct strings dynamically by combining fixed text with dynamic data.

Python provides several ways to perform string formatting:

Using % Operator (Old Style Formatting): This method involves using placeholders with **%** followed by a tuple of values to be inserted into the placeholders.

Example:

```
name = "Alice"
age = 30
message = "Hello, my name is %s and I am %d years old." % (name, age)
print(message)  # Output: "Hello, my name is Alice and I am 30 years old."
```

Using str.format(): The format() method allows you to create a string with placeholders enclosed in curly braces {}. You can then call the format() method and provide the values to replace the placeholders.

Example:

```
name = "Alice"
age = 30
message = "Hello, my name is {} and I am {} years old.".format(name, age)
print(message)  # Output: "Hello, my name is Alice and I am 30 years old."
```

Using f-strings (Formatted String Literals): Introduced in Python 3.6, f-strings provide a concise and readable way to perform string formatting. You can include expressions inside curly braces {} directly within the string, and they will be evaluated and replaced with their values.

Example:

```
name = "Alice"
age = 30
message = f"Hello, my name is {name} and I am {age} years old."
print(message)  # Output: "Hello, my name is Alice and I am 30 years old."
```

String formatting is particularly useful when you want to include dynamic values within a string, such as variable values, results of calculations, or user inputs. It improves code readability and maintainability by allowing you to construct complex strings without excessive concatenation.

4.7. Escape Character

An escape character in Python is a special character that is used to signal the interpreter that the following character(s) should be treated in a special way. Escape characters are preceded by a backslash \. They are used to represent characters that would otherwise be difficult to include in a string or might have a different interpretation within the string.

Here are some common escape characters in Python:

Escape Sequence	**Description**
\\	Backslash (\)
\'	Single quote (')

Escape Sequence	Description
\"	Double quote (")
\n	Newline
\t	Tab
\r	Carriage return
\b	Backspace
\f	Form feed
\ooo	Character with octal value ooo
\xhh	Character with hex value hh

\n: Newline - inserts a new line.
Example:
```
text = "Hello\nWorld"
print(text)
# Output:
# Hello
# World
```

\t: Tab - inserts a horizontal tab.
```
text = "Hello\tWorld"
print(text)
# Output: Hello    World
```

\' and \": Single and Double Quotes - allows you to include single or double quotes within a string.
Example:
```
single_quoted = 'He said, "Hello!"'
double_quoted = "She said, 'Hi!'"
```

\\: Backslash - inserts a literal backslash.
```
text = "This is a backslash: \\"
print(text)
# Output: This is a backslash: \
```

\b: Backspace - moves the cursor back one character, removing the preceding character.
Example:
```
text = "Hello\bWorld"
print(text)
# Output: HellWorld
```

\r: Carriage Return - moves the cursor to the beginning of the line.
Example:
```
text = "Hello\rWorld"
print(text)
```

Output: World

\n: Unicode Escape - allows you to insert Unicode characters using their hexadecimal value.
Example:
unicode_char = "\u03B1" # Greek letter alpha (α)
Escape characters are particularly useful when you want to include special characters, control formatting, or create strings with specific properties. They ensure that characters are interpreted as intended within the string.

4.8. Assigning a string to a variable

Assigning a string to a variable in Python is a straightforward process. You simply use the assignment operator = to associate the string value with the variable name. Here's how you can do it:

```
# Assigning a string to a variable
my_string = "Hello, World!"
# Printing the variable to verify the assignment
print(my_string)
```

In this example, the variable **my_string** is assigned the value **"Hello, World!"**. You can then use this variable throughout your code to reference and manipulate the string.

Keep in mind that variable names in Python are case-sensitive, meaning that **my_string**, **My_String**, and **MY_STRING** would all be considered different variable names. It's good practice to use descriptive and meaningful names for your variables to make your code more understandable.

Example 1

```
str = "HELLO"
str[0] = "h"
print(str)
```

Output:

```
Traceback (most recent call last):
  File "12.py", line 2, in <module>
    str[0] = "h";
TypeError: 'str' object does not support item assignment
```

However, in example 1, the string **str** can be assigned completely to a new content as specified in the following example.

Example 2

```
str = "HELLO"
print(str)
str = "hello"
print(str)
```

Output:

```
HELLO
hello
```

4.9. Deleting Strings in Python

Strings are immutable in Python, which means you can't directly delete or remove individual characters from a String. However, you can delete an entire string using the **del** keyword. Here's how:

```
# Deleting an entire string
my_string = "Hello, World!"
del my_string
```

After this, trying to print my_string would result in a NameErrorIt's important to note that once you delete a string using **del**, you can't access that variable anymore, and trying to do so will raise a **NameError**.In your example, you attempted to use **del** to remove a character from a string:

```
str = "JAVATPOINT"
del str[1]
# This would result in a TypeError since you can't delete individual characters from a string
```

To sum it up, you can use **del** to remove an entire string variable, but you cannot use it to delete specific characters from a string due to their immutability.

4.10. Reassigning Strings

Reassigning values to a string in Python involves modifying an existing string variable by assigning it a new value. Since strings are immutable, you cannot change the characters within an existing string directly. Instead, you create a new string with the desired modifications and associate it with the same variable name. Here's how string reassignment works in detail:

1. Basic Reassignment: You can simply assign a new value to a string variable, overwriting the previous value.

```
text = "Hello"text = "Hi"  # Reassigning the value of 'text'
print(text)  # Output: "Hi"
```

2. Concatenation for Reassignment: You can reassign a string by concatenating it with other strings or variables.

```
name = "Alice"
greeting = "Hello, " + name  # Concatenating to reassign
print(greeting)  # Output: "Hello, Alice"
```

3. Using String Methods: You can use string methods to modify a string and then reassign it.

```
message = "   Hello, World!   "
message = message.strip()  # Removing spaces and reassigning
print(message)  # Output: "Hello, World!"
```

4. Reassignment with Formatting: You can also reassign by using string formatting techniques.

```
name = "Bob"
age = 25
message = "My name is {} and I am {} years old.".format(name, age)
print(message)  # Output: "My name is Bob and I am 25 years old."
```

5. Reassignment with f-strings: Using f-strings, you can reassign a string variable while including dynamic values.

```
name = "Charlie"
greeting = f"Hi, my name is {name}"
print(greeting)  # Output: "Hi, my name is Charlie"
```

Remember that when reassigning a string, you're creating a new string object in memory and associating it with the variable. The old string is discarded if there are no other references to it, and Python's garbage collector will eventually clean up unused memory.

Reassigning strings is a crucial aspect of working with text data in Python. It allows you to modify and transform strings to achieve desired outputs.

4.11. Python string function

In Python, a function is a reusable block of code that performs a specific task or set of tasks. It's a way to organize and encapsulate logic, making the code more modular, readable, and maintainable. Functions take input arguments (if needed), perform operations on them, and often return a result.

Key features of functions in Python include:

Reusability: Once defined, functions can be called multiple times from different parts of the code, eliminating the need to repeat the same code.

Modularity: Functions allow you to break down a complex task into smaller, manageable pieces of code. This improves code organization and makes it easier to debug and maintain.

Abstraction: Functions abstract away the implementation details. You only need to know what a function does and what inputs it requires, not how it accomplishes the task.

Arguments: Functions can accept zero or more arguments. These arguments are passed to the function when it's called and provide the necessary data for the function to operate.

Return Value: Functions can return values back to the caller. The return value can be used for further calculations or operations.

len(): Returns the length (number of characters) of a string.

```
my_string = "Hello, World!"
length = len(my_string)
print(length)  # Output: 13
```

upper() and lower(): Converts the string to uppercase or lowercase, respectively.

```
text = "Python is Fun"
uppercase_text = text.upper()
lowercase_text = text.lower()
```

str.capitalize() and str.title(): Capitalizes the first character or each word in the string.

```
text = "hello world"
capital_text = text.capitalize()  # "Hello world"
title_text = text.title()  # "Hello World"
```

str.strip(), str.lstrip(), and str.rstrip(): Removes leading/trailing spaces or specific characters.

```
text = "   Spaces   "
stripped_text = text.strip()  # "Spaces"
left_stripped = text.lstrip()  # "Spaces   "
right_stripped = text.rstrip()  # "   Spaces"
```

str.replace(old, new): Replaces occurrences of a substring with another substring.

```
text = "I like apples"
new_text = text.replace("apples", "bananas")  # "I like bananas"
```

str.split(delimiter): Splits the string into a list of substrings based on a delimiter.

```
text = "apple,banana,orange"
fruits = text.split(",")  # ['apple', 'banana', 'orange']
```

str.join(iterable): Joins elements of an iterable into a string using the specified string as a separator.

```
fruits = ['apple', 'banana', 'orange']
combined = ", ".join(fruits)  # "apple, banana, orange"
```

str.find(substring) and str.rfind(substring): Searches for the first/last occurrence of a substring and returns its index. If not found, returns -1.

```
text = "Hello, World!"
index = text.find("World")  # 7
r_index = text.rfind("l")  # 10 (last 'l')
```

str.startswith(prefix) and str.endswith(suffix): Checks if the string starts or ends with a specific prefix or suffix.

```
text = "Hello, World!"
starts_with = text.startswith("Hello")  # True
ends_with = text.endswith("!")  # True
```

str.count(substring): Counts the number of occurrences of a substring in the string.

```
text = "hello, hello world"
count = text.count("hello")  # 2
```

These string functions are immensely useful for various tasks involving string manipulation, validation, and analysis in Python. They help you work with text data efficiently and effectively.

Summary

Strings in Python are used to represent a sequence of characters and are declared either using single quotes ('string') or double quotes ("string"). Strings are immutable, meaning once they are created, they cannot be changed.

In Python, strings are sequences of characters enclosed in quotes, either single (' ') or double (" "). They are immutable, meaning that once created, individual characters within them cannot be changed. You can, however, concatenate strings, slice them, and create new strings from existing ones. Python supports a variety of string methods for manipulation, such as upper(), lower(), strip(), replace(), etc.

Strings support indexing, and you can access individual characters using square brackets, with indices starting at zero. Slicing allows you to obtain sub-strings: my_string[1:4] will give you characters from index 1 up to, but not including, index 4.

String formatting is a powerful feature in Python. The older % formatting and .format() methods are still in use, but f-strings, introduced in Python 3.6, offer a more concise and readable way to include variables in strings. For example, f"Hello, {name}!" embeds the variable name within a greeting.

Special characters like newlines (\n) and tabs (\t) can be included in strings with escape sequences. Triple quotes (''' ''' or """ """) are used for multi-line strings.

Strings can also be converted to other data types and vice versa. For example, you can use int() to convert a numeric string to an integer, and str() to convert an integer to a string.

Strings are versatile and essential data types in Python, offering a wide variety of built-in methods and functionalities for efficient string manipulation. From basic string creation and concatenation to advanced formatting and encoding, Python's string capabilities make it easy to work with text data.

Exercise 1:

Multiple Choice Questions (MCQs):

Question 1: In Python, how are strings defined?

a) Using single quotes (')

b) Using double quotes (")
c) Using either single or double quotes
d) Using triple quotes (''' or """)

Question 2: What will **len("Python")** return?
a) 6
b) 5
c) 7
d) "Python"

Question 3: Which method is used to convert a string to uppercase in Python?
a) to_upper()
b) uppercase()
c) upper()
d) case_upper()

Question 4: What will **"Hello, " + "world!"** evaluate to?
a) "Hello, world!"
b) "Hello, world!"
c) "Hello, "world!"
d) Error

Question 5: How can you access the character at index 3 in a string **text**?
a) text[3]
b) text.char(3)
c) text.get(3)
d) text.substring(3)

Question 6: Which method is used to find the index of the first occurrence of a substring in a string?
a) index()
b) find()
c) search()
d) locate()

Question 7: Which escape sequence is used to insert a newline character in a string?
a) **\n**
b) **\r**
c) **\t**
d) **\b**

Question 8: What does the method **strip()** do for a string in Python?
a) Removes all spaces from the beginning and end of the string.
b) Converts the string to uppercase.
c) Splits the string into a list.
d) Replaces all occurrences of a substring.

Answers

1. c 2. a 3. c 4. a 5. a 6. b 7. a 8. a

Exercise 2:

True/False Questions:

Question 1: In Python, strings are mutable, meaning their content can be changed after creation.
Question 2: The **str()** function can be used to convert a non-string object to a string.
Question 3: The **replace()** method changes all occurrences of a substring in a string.
Question 4: Strings in Python can be indexed from 0 to the length of the string minus one.
Question 5: The **split()** method splits a string into a list of substrings based on a specified delimiter.

Answer

1. False 2. True 3. True 4. True 5. True

Exercise 3:

Review questions:

Question 1: What is a string in Python and how is it created?
Question 2: How do you access individual characters in a string?

Question 3: What does it mean for strings to be immutable?
Question 4: How do you concatenate two or more strings?
Question 5: How do you find the length of a string without using any built-in functions?
Question 6: What are escape characters, and how are they used in strings?
Question 7: What is string slicing and how is it different from indexing?
Question 8: How do you reverse a string in Python?
Question 9: What are some common string methods for case manipulation?
Question 10: How do you convert other data types to strings?
Question 11: How do you split a string into a list of substrings?
Question 12: What does the join method do in the context of strings?
Question 13: How do you find the occurrence of a substring within a string?
Question 14: What is the difference between strip(), rstrip(), and lstrip() methods?
Question 15: How do you format strings using f-strings or the format() method?
Question 16: How do you compare two strings in Python?
Question 17: What is string interpolation, and how is it performed in Python?
Question 18: How do you concatenate a string with a non-string type?
Question 19: What are raw strings and how are they useful?
Question 20: How do you check if a string starts or ends with a specific substring?

Chapter 5

Operators in Python

Operators in Python are special symbols or keywords that are used to perform various operations on variables or values. They define how variables and values interact with each other, allowing you to perform calculations, comparisons, assignments, and more. Python supports a wide range of operators, each designed for specific tasks. Here are some common types of operators in Python:

- Arithmetic operators
- Assignment operators
- Comparison operators
- Logical operators
- Identity operators
- Membership operators
- Bitwise operators

In Python, operators are the building blocks that help you manipulate data and control the flow of your programs. They are versatile tools that can be applied in a multitude of scenarios, from simple calculations to complex logical operations.

One important category to note is the arithmetic operators, which include the familiar addition, subtraction, multiplication, and division, as well as some less common operations like modulo and exponentiation. These allow you to perform mathematical operations directly within your code.

Assignment operators extend beyond the basic equal sign. Python also offers shorthand ways to update a variable's value relative to its current value, like += for addition or *= for multiplication. These make your code more concise while maintaining readability.

Comparison operators are crucial for decision-making in code. They allow you to compare two variables and determine the relational condition between them. These operators return boolean values, enabling them to be used in control structures like if and while statements.

Logical operators are another essential set, particularly and, or, and not. They are key to constructing complex conditional statements and are commonly used in conjunction with comparison operators.

Identity operators like is and is not compare the memory locations of two variables, not just their content. This is useful for checking if two variables refer to the same object, rather than just having the same value.

Membership operators (in and not in) let you check for the existence of a value within a sequence or other iterable data types. This is particularly helpful when working with lists, tuples, or dictionaries.

Bitwise operators are specialized tools for manipulating individual bits within an integer. They are mainly used in low-level programming and specific algorithms where bit manipulation is necessary.

To sum it up, operators in Python serve as the linchpin for carrying out a wide array of operations. They make it easier to write efficient, readable, and functional code, allowing you to express complex operations and logic in a succinct manner.

5.1 Python Arithmetic Operators

Arithmetic operators are used with numeric values to perform common mathematical operations:

Operator	Name	Example
+	Addition	x + y
-	Subtraction	x - y
*	Multiplication	x * y
/	Division	x / y
%	Modulus	x % y
**	Exponentiation	x ** y

//	Floor division	x // y

Arithmetic operators in programming are used to perform various mathematical operations on numerical values. Python, like many other programming languages, provides a set of arithmetic operators that allow you to perform addition, subtraction, multiplication, division, and more. Here's an explanation of each arithmetic operator in detail:

Addition (+): Adds two operands together.

```
a = 5
b = 3
result = a + b  # 5 + 3 = 8
```

Subtraction (-): Subtracts the second number from the first.

```
x = 10
y = 7
difference = x - y  # 10 - 7 = 3
print(difference)  # Output: 3
```

Multiplication (*): Multiplies two numbers.

```
p = 4
q = 6
product = p * q  # 4 * 6 = 24
print(product)  # Output: 24
```

Integer Division (//): Divides the first number by the second and returns an integer result (floor division).

```
dividend = 17
divisor = 4
int_quotient = dividend // divisor  # 17 // 4 = 4
print(int_quotient)              # Output: 4
```

Modulus (%): Returns the remainder of the division of the first number by the second.

```
dividend = 17
divisor = 4
remainder = dividend % divisor  # 17 % 4 = 1
print(remainder)              # Output: 1
```

Exponentiation ()**: Raises the first number to the power of the second.

```
base = 2
exponent = 3
result = base ** exponent  # 2 ** 3 = 8
print(result)            # Output: 8
```

Combining these operators can yield more complex expressions:

```
expression = (5 + 3) * (10 / 2) + 7
# (8) * (5.0) + 7
# 40.0 + 7
# Result: 47.0
print(expression) # Output: 47.0
```

These examples demonstrate how arithmetic operators are used in Python to perform basic mathematical operations. Keep in mind that Python follows the standard order of operations (PEMDAS/BODMAS) when evaluating complex expressions, meaning that operations inside parentheses are evaluated first, followed by exponentiation, multiplication and division, and finally addition and subtraction.

5.2 Python Assignment Operators

Assignment operators are used to assign values to variables:

Operator	Example	Same As
=	x = 5	x = 5
+=	x += 3	x = x + 3
-=	x -= 3	x = x - 3
*=	x *= 3	x = x * 3

<table>
<tr><td>/=</td><td>x /= 3</td><td>x = x / 3</td></tr>
<tr><td>%=</td><td>x %= 3</td><td>x = x % 3</td></tr>
<tr><td>//=</td><td>x //= 3</td><td>x = x // 3</td></tr>
<tr><td>**=</td><td>x **= 3</td><td>x = x ** 3</td></tr>
<tr><td>&=</td><td>x &= 3</td><td>x = x & 3</td></tr>
<tr><td>|=</td><td>x |= 3</td><td>x = x | 3</td></tr>
<tr><td>^=</td><td>x ^= 3</td><td>x = x ^ 3</td></tr>
<tr><td>>>=</td><td>x >>= 3</td><td>x = x >> 3</td></tr>
<tr><td><<=</td><td>x <<= 3</td><td>x = x << 3</td></tr>
</table>

Assignment operators in Python are used to assign values to variables. They allow you to perform an operation and assign the result back to the variable. Here are the assignment operators in Python along with examples for each:

Assignment (=): Assigns the value on the right to the variable on the left.

```
x = 5
y = x
print(y)  # Output: 5
```

Addition Assignment (+=): Adds the value on the right to the variable on the left and assigns the result back to the variable.

```
a = 10
a += 3  # Equivalent to a = a + 3
print(a)  # Output: 13
```

Subtraction Assignment (-=): Subtracts the value on the right from the variable on the left and assigns the result back to the variable.

```
b = 7
b -= 2  # Equivalent to b = b - 2
print(b)  # Output: 5
```

Multiplication Assignment (*=): Multiplies the variable on the left by the value on the right and assigns the result back to the variable.

```
c = 4
c *= 2  # Equivalent to c = c * 2
print(c)  # Output: 8
```

Division Assignment (/=): Divides the variable on the left by the value on the right and assigns the result back to the variable.

```
d = 15
d /= 3  # Equivalent to d = d / 3
print(d)  # Output: 5.0
```

Integer Division Assignment (//=): Performs integer division of the variable on the left by the value on the right and assigns the result back to the variable.

```
e = 17
e //= 4  # Equivalent to e = e // 4
print(e)  # Output: 4
```

Modulus Assignment (%=): Computes the remainder of the division of the variable on the left by the value on the right and assigns the result back to the variable.

```
f = 17
f %= 4  # Equivalent to f = f % 4
print(f)  # Output: 1
```

Exponentiation Assignment (=)**: Raises the variable on the left to the power of the value on the right and assigns the result back to the variable.

```
g = 2
g **= 3  # Equivalent to g = g ** 3
print(g)  # Output: 8
```

These assignment operators are shortcuts for performing an operation and assigning the result back to the same variable. They can make your code more concise and readable when you need to update variables based on some calculation.

5.3 Python Comparison Operators

Comparison operators are used to compare two values:

Operator	Name	Example
==	Equal	x == y
!=	Not equal	x != y
>	Greater than	x > y
<	Less than	x < y
>=	Greater than or equal to	x >= y
<=	Less than or equal to	x <= y

Comparison operators in Python are used to compare two values and determine the relationship between them. These operators return Boolean values (True or False) based on whether the comparison is true or false. Here are the comparison operators in Python, along with explanations and examples for each:

Equal to (==): Checks if two values are equal.

```
x = 5
y = 5
result = x == y  # True, because 5 is equal to 5
print(result)   # Output: True
```

Not Equal to (!=): Checks if two values are not equal.

```
a = 10
b = 7
result = a != b  # True, because 10 is not equal to 7
print(result)   # Output: True
```

Greater than (>): Checks if the left value is greater than the right value.

```
p = 15
q = 10
result = p > q  # True, because 15 is greater than 10
print(result)#The output is : True
```

Less than (<): Checks if the left value is less than the right value.

```
m = 5
n = 8
result = m < n  # True, because 5 is less than 8
print(result)  # Output: True
```

Greater than or equal to (>=): Checks if the left value is greater than or equal to the right value.

```
i = 20
j = 20
result = i >= j  # True, because 20 is equal to 20
print(result)   # Output: True
```

Less than or equal to (<=): Checks if the left value is less than or equal to the right value.

```
r = 25
```

```
s = 30
result = r <= s  # True, because 25 is less than 30
print(result)   # Output: True
```

These comparison operators are used to evaluate expressions and conditions in various programming contexts. For example, you might use them in conditional statements (if, elif, else) to control the flow of your program based on the comparison results. Keep in mind that comparison operators are not to be confused with the assignment operator (=), which is used to assign values to variables.

5.4 Python Logical Operators

Logical operators are used to combine conditional statements:

Operator	Description	Example
and	Returns True if both statements are true	x < 5 and x < 10
or	Returns True if one of the statements is true	x < 5 or x < 4
not	Reverse the result, returns False if the result is true	not(x < 5 and x < 10)

Logical operators in Python are used to combine or manipulate Boolean values. They allow you to create more complex conditions by combining multiple Boolean expressions. There are three logical operators in Python: **and**, **or**, and **not**. Here's an explanation of each with examples:

Logical AND (and): Returns **True** if both operands are **True**, otherwise, it returns **False**.

```
x = True
y = False
result = x and y  # False, because both x and y are not True
print(result)   # Output: False
```

Logical OR (or): Returns **True** if at least one of the operands is **True**, otherwise, it returns **False**.

```
a = True
b = False
result = a or b  # True, because at least one of a and b is True
print(result)   # Output: True
```

Logical NOT (not): Returns the opposite Boolean value of the operand. If the operand is **True**, it returns **False**, and vice versa.

```
p = True
q = False
result_p = not p  # False, because not True is False
result_q = not q  # True, because not False is True
print(result_p)  # Output: False
print(result_q)  # Output: True
```

You can also combine logical operators to create more complex conditions:

```
num = 7
result = (num > 5) and (num < 10)  # True, because num is greater than 5 and less than 10
print(result) # Output: True
```

These logical operators are frequently used in conditional statements (**if**, **elif**, **else**) and loops to control the flow of your program based on conditions. By using logical operators, you can create expressions that involve multiple conditions and make your code more versatile and powerful.

5.5 Python Identity Operators

Identity operators are used to compare the objects, not if they are equal, but if they are actually the same object, with the same memory location:

Operator	Description	Example

is	Returns True if both variables are the same object	x is y
is not	Returns True if both variables are not the same object	x is not y

Identity is Operator:

The is operator returns True if both operands reference the same object in memory.

```
# Example 1
x = [1, 2, 3]
y = x
result1 = x is y
print(result1)  # Output: True

# Example 2
a = "hello"
b = "hello"
result2 = a is b
print(result2)  # Output: True

# Example 3
m = 10
n = 10
result3 = m is n
print(result3)  # Output: True
```

In these examples, **result1** is **True** because both **x** and **y** reference the same list object. Similarly, **result2** and **result3** are **True** because both **a** and **b**, and both **m** and **n**, respectively, reference the same string and integer objects due to Python's object caching mechanism.

Identity is not Operator:

The **is not** operator returns **True** if both operands do not reference the same object in memory.

```
# Example 1
p = [1, 2, 3]
q = [1, 2, 3]
result4 = p is not q
print(result4)  # Output: True

# Example 2
c = "world"
d = "hello"
result5 = c is not d
print(result5)  # Output: True

# Example 3
x = 5
y = 6
result6 = x is not y
print(result6)  # Output: True
```

In these examples, **result4** is **True** because **p** and **q** reference different list objects, **result5** is **True** because **c** and **d** reference different string objects, and **result6** is **True** because **x** and **y** reference different integer objects.

Remember that the identity operators compare the memory locations of objects, not their content. They are often used to check whether two variables reference the same instance of an object, especially when working with mutable objects like lists or instances of user-defined classes.

5.6 Python Membership Operators

Membership operators are used to test if a sequence is presented in an object:

Operator	**Description**	**Example**

in	Returns True if a sequence with the specified value is present in the object	x in y
not in	Returns True if a sequence with the specified value is not present in the object	x not in y

Membership operators in Python are used to check whether a value is a member of a sequence, such as a string, list, tuple, or set. They return **True** if the value is found in the sequence and **False** otherwise. There are two membership operators in Python: **in** and **not in**. Here's an explanation of each with examples:

Membership in Operator:

The in operator returns True if a value is found in the sequence, and False if it's not found.

```
# Example 1
text = "Hello, World!"
result1 = "Hello" in text
print(result1)  # Output: True

# Example 2
numbers = [1, 2, 3, 4, 5]
result2 = 3 in numbers
print(result2)  # Output: True

# Example 3
fruits = ("apple", "banana", "cherry")
result3 = "orange" in fruits
print(result3)  # Output: False
```

In these examples, **result1** is **True** because the substring "Hello" is present in the string **text**, **result2** is **True** because the number **3** is present in the list **numbers**, and **result3** is **False** because the string "orange" is not present in the tuple **fruits**.

Non-Membership not in Operator:

The **not in** operator returns **True** if a value is not found in the sequence, and **False** if it's found.

```
# Example 1
word = "Python"
result4 = "java" not in word
print(result4)  # Output: True

# Example 2
grades = {"Alice": 95, "Bob": 82, "Charlie": 75}
result5 = "Charlie" not in grades
print(result5)  # Output: False

# Example 3
letters = ['a', 'b', 'c']
result6 = 'd' not in letters
print(result6)  # Output: True
```

In these examples, **result4** is **True** because the substring "java" is not present in the string **word**, **result5** is **False** because the key "Charlie" is present in the dictionary **grades**, and **result6** is **True** because the letter **'d'** is not present in the list **letters**.

Membership operators are useful when you want to check if a value exists in a collection or sequence before performing further actions. They are commonly used in conditional statements to control the flow of your program based on whether a value is present or not.

5.7 Python Bitwise Operators

Bitwise operators are used to compare (binary) numbers:

Operator	**Name**	**Description**	**Example**

&	AND	Sets each bit to 1 if both bits are 1	x & y
|	OR	Sets each bit to 1 if one of two bits is 1	x | y
^	XOR	Sets each bit to 1 if only one of two bits is 1	x ^ y
~	NOT	Inverts all the bits	~x
<<	Zero fill left shift	Shift left by pushing zeros in from the right and let the leftmost bits fall off	x << 2
>>	Signed right shift	Shift right by pushing copies of the leftmost bit in from the left, and let the rightmost bits fall off	x >> 2

Bitwise operators in Python are used to perform bit-level operations on integer values. These operators manipulate individual bits within the binary representation of the numbers. There are six bitwise operators in Python: **&** (AND), | (OR), ^ (XOR), ~ (NOT), << (left shift), and >> (right shift). Let's explore each of them in detail with examples:

Bitwise AND (&): Performs a bitwise AND operation between corresponding bits of two integers. A bit is set in the result only if the corresponding bits of both operands are set.

```
a = 5  # 0b0101 in binary
b = 3  # 0b0011 in binary
result_and = a & b
print(result_and)  # Output: 1 (0b0001 in binary)
```

Bitwise OR (|): Performs a bitwise OR operation between corresponding bits of two integers. A bit is set in the result if either of the corresponding bits of the operands is set.

```
x = 5  # 0b0101 in binary
y = 3  # 0b0011 in binary
result_or = x | y
print(result_or)  # Output: 7 (0b0111 in binary)
```

Bitwise XOR (^): Performs a bitwise XOR (exclusive OR) operation between corresponding bits of two integers. A bit is set in the result if the corresponding bits of the operands are different.

```
m = 5  # 0b0101 in binary
n = 3  # 0b0011 in binary
result_xor = m ^ n
print(result_xor)  # Output: 6 (0b0110 in binary)
```

Bitwise NOT (~): Flips the bits of an integer, resulting in the one's complement of the number. Note that this operation can vary due to how negative numbers are represented.

```
num = 5  # 0b00000101 in binary
result_not = ~num
print(result_not)  # Output: -6 (assuming 2's complement representation)
```

Left Shift (<<): Shifts the bits of an integer to the left by a specified number of positions. The leftmost bits are lost, and zeros are filled in on the right.

```
p = 5  # 0b0101 in binary
shifted_left = p << 2
print(shifted_left)  # Output: 20 (0b10100 in binary)
```

5.8 Operator Precedence

Operator precedence describes the order in which operations are performed.

The precedence order is described in the table below, starting with the highest precedence at the top:

Operator	Description
()	Parentheses

**	
+x -x ~x	Unary plus, unary minus, and bitwise NOT
* / // %	Multiplication, division, floor division, and modulus
+ -	Addition and subtraction
<< >>	Bitwise left and right shifts
&	Bitwise AND
^	Bitwise XOR
|	Bitwise OR
== != > >= < <= is is not in not in	Comparisons, identity, and membership operators
not	Logical NOT
and	AND
or	OR

Operator precedence in Python refers to the rules that determine the order in which different operators are evaluated when an expression involves multiple operators. These rules ensure that expressions are evaluated consistently and produce the expected results. Operator precedence helps avoid ambiguity in complex expressions and dictates the sequence in which operations are performed.

Python follows the PEMDAS/BODMAS rule, which stands for Parentheses/Brackets, Exponents/Orders, Multiplication and Division, and Addition and Subtraction. This rule is also known as the order of operations. It ensures that operations inside parentheses are evaluated first, followed by exponentiation, then multiplication and division (from left to right), and finally addition and subtraction (from left to right).

For example:

```
result = 3 + 4 * 5  # Multiplication before addition: 3 + (4 * 5) = 23
```

If you want to override the default order of operations, you can use parentheses to explicitly group expressions:

```
result = (3 + 4) * 5  # Addition before multiplication: (3 + 4) * 5 = 35
```

When expressions involve multiple operators of the same precedence level, the evaluation order depends on their associativity. Most operators in Python are left-associative, meaning they are evaluated from left to right. For example, in **5 - 3 - 1**, the subtraction operations are performed from left to right: **(5 - 3) - 1 = 1**.

It's important to note that different operators have different precedence levels. For instance, multiplication and division have higher precedence than addition and subtraction. Logical operators have lower precedence than arithmetic operators. To ensure that your expressions are evaluated as intended, it's crucial to be aware of the precedence and associativity of the operators you're using.

In situations where the precedence and associativity might lead to confusion, it's a good practice to use parentheses to explicitly define the order of operations. This not only makes your code more readable but also avoids potential errors. Overall, understanding operator precedence is fundamental to writing correct and efficient Python code, especially when dealing with complex expressions involving multiple operators.
Top of Form

Summary

In Python, operators are symbols that perform operations on one or more operands (values or variables). They allow you to manipulate data in various ways, such as performing arithmetic calculations, comparing values, and more. Here's a summary of the different types of operators in Python:

Comparison Operators:

- Equal to (==): Checks if two operands are equal.
- Not equal to (!=): Checks if two operands are not equal.
- Greater than (>): Checks if the first operand is greater than the second.
- Less than (<): Checks if the first operand is less than the second.
- Greater than or equal to (>=): Checks if the first operand is greater than or equal to the second.
- Less than or equal to (<=): Checks if the first operand is less than or equal to the second.

Logical Operators:

- and: Returns True if both operands are True.
- or: Returns True if at least one operand is True.
- not: Returns the logical negation of an operand.

Assignment Operators:

- =: Assigns the value on the right to the variable on the left.
- +=: Adds the right operand to the left operand and assigns the result to the left operand.
- -=: Subtracts the right operand from the left operand and assigns the result to the left operand.
- *=: Multiplies the left operand by the right operand and assigns the result to the left operand.
- /=: Divides the left operand by the right operand and assigns the result to the left operand.
- %=: Calculates the modulus of the left operand with the right operand and assigns the result to the left operand.
- //=: Performs floor division and assigns the result to the left operand.
- **=: Raises the left operand to the power of the right operand and assigns the result to the left operand.

Arithmetic Operators:

- Addition (+): Adds two operands.
- Subtraction (-): Subtracts the second operand from the first.
- Multiplication (*): Multiplies two operands.
- Division (/): Divides the first operand by the second (returns a float).
- Floor Division (//): Divides and truncates the result to an integer.
- Modulus (%): Returns the remainder of division.
- Exponentiation (**): Raises the first operand to the power of the second.

Bitwise Operators (operate on individual bits):

- &: Bitwise AND
- |: Bitwise OR
- ^: Bitwise XOR
- ~: Bitwise NOT
- <<: Left shift
- : Right shift

Membership Operators:

- in: Returns True if a value is found in a sequence.
- not in: Returns True if a value is not found in a sequence.

Identity Operators:

- is: Returns True if two operands reference the same object.
- is not: Returns True if two operands do not reference the same object.

These operators are essential for performing a wide range of operations and calculations in Python.

Exercise 1:

Multiple Choice Questions (MCQs):

Question 1: Which operator is used for exponentiation in Python?

a) **
b) ^
c) ^^
d) *^

Question 2: What is the result of **15 / 2** in Python?

a) 7
b) 7.5
c) 7.0
d) 8

Question 3: Which operator is used to perform floor division in Python?

a) //
b) %
c) %%
d) /

Question 4: What does the modulo operator (%) do?

a) Returns the quotient of division
b) Returns the remainder of division
c) Returns the product of two numbers
d) Returns the square root of a number

Question 5: What is the result of **"Hello"** + **"World"**?

a) "Hello World"
b) "Hello + World"
c) Error
d) "HelloWorld"

Question 6: What is the purpose of the == operator in Python?

a) Checks if two variables are equal
b) Assigns a value to a variable
c) Performs mathematical addition
d) Checks if two variables are not equal

Question 7: Which operator is used to check if a value is not in a sequence?

a) is not
b) not in
c) !==
d) !=

Question 8: What is the order of precedence of operators in Python?

a) Parentheses > Exponentiation > Multiplication/Division > Addition/Subtraction
b) Exponentiation > Parentheses > Multiplication/Division > Addition/Subtraction
c) Parentheses > Multiplication/Division > Addition/Subtraction > Exponentiation
d) Exponentiation > Multiplication/Division > Addition/Subtraction > Parentheses

Answer

1. a 2. b 3.a 4.b 5.d 6.a 7.b 8.a

Exercise 2:

True/False Questions:

Question 1: The += operator is used for subtraction in Python.

Question 2: The **and** operator returns **True** if at least one of the operands is

Question 3: The **not** operator is used to negate the value of a boolean expression.

Question 4: The == operator compares the values of two variables and their data types.

Question 5: The **is** operator is used to check if two variables have the same value.

Answer

1. False 2. False 3. True 4. False 5. False

Exercise 3:

Review questions:

Question 1: What are operators in Python and what is their basic function?

Question 2: How are arithmetic operators different from comparison operators?

Question 3: What does the += operator do in Python?

Question 4: Can you explain the difference between == and is operators?

Question 5: What is the role of logical operators like and, or, and not?

Question 6: How is the modulus operator % used, and what does it return?

Question 7: What are bitwise operators, and can you name a few?

Question 8: How do you perform exponentiation using operators in Python?

Question 9: What is operator precedence, and how does it affect an expression's outcome?

Question 10: What does the floor division operator // do?

Question 11: How is the ternary operator used in Python?

Question 12: What are identity operators, and what do they check?

Question 13: What is the difference between += and =+ in Python?

Question 14: How do assignment operators like *=, -=, and /= work?

Question 15: What does the in operator check for when used with collections like lists or strings?

Question 16: Can you use arithmetic operators with strings? If so, give an example.

Question 17: What are the limitations of using the not operator in Python?

Question 18: What is the significance of parentheses () in complex expressions involving multiple operators?

Question 19: How do the << and >> bitwise operators function?

Question 20: What is the ** operator used for, and how does it differ from ^?

Chapter 6

Python Data Structure

Data structures are fundamental concepts in computer science and programming that allow you to organize and store data efficiently based on specific requirements. They provide a framework for managing and manipulating data, making it easier to perform operations, access, and modify information in various scenarios. In Python, the concept of data structures is well-supported and provides a simple and versatile way to work with different types of data.

Python offers a variety of built-in data structures that cater to different use cases and scenarios. These data structures include:

Lists: Ordered collections of elements that can be of different data types. Lists are mutable, which means you can add, remove, and modify elements easily.

Tuples: Similar to lists but immutable, meaning their elements cannot be changed after creation. Tuples are often used when you want to ensure data integrity.

Dictionaries: Key-value pairs that allow you to store and retrieve data based on unique keys. Dictionaries are useful for fast lookups and mapping relationships.

Sets: Unordered collections of unique elements. Sets are helpful for finding unique values, performing mathematical set operations, and removing duplicates.

Python also supports advanced data structures like trees, graphs, stacks, queues, and more. These data structures can be implemented using the built-in data structures or custom implementations.

Python's simplicity and expressive syntax make it an ideal language for learning and working with data structures. The built-in functions and methods associated with these structures simplify common operations. Python's dynamic typing allows you to create heterogeneous data structures, where different types of data can be stored together.

Learning about data structures in Python is essential for developing efficient and well-organized programs. Choosing the right data structure for a specific problem can significantly impact the performance and readability of your code. By understanding and utilizing Python's data structures effectively, you can write cleaner, more maintainable, and more performant code.

6.1 List indexing and splitting

List indexing and splitting are essential concepts in Python when working with lists. Let's go through both of them in detail with examples.

List Indexing: Indexing in Python refers to accessing individual elements within a list by their position. Lists in Python are zero-indexed, which means the first element has an index of 0, the second element has an index of 1, and so on. You can also use negative indexing, where -1 represents the last element, -2 represents the second-to-last element, and so on.

```
my_list = [10, 20, 30, 40, 50]

# Accessing elements using positive indexing
first_element = my_list[0]  # 10
second_element = my_list[1] # 20
# Accessing elements using negative indexing
last_element = my_list[-1]  # 50
second_to_last = my_list[-2] # 40

print(first_element, second_element, last_element, second_to_last)
```

List Splitting: List splitting involves extracting a portion of a list to create a new list. This can be done using slicing, where you specify the starting and ending indices. The slice includes all elements from the starting index up to, but not including, the ending index.

```
my_list = [10, 20, 30, 40, 50]
# Slicing to create a new list
sub_list = my_list[1:4] # [20, 30, 40]
```

If you omit the starting index, Python assumes it's the beginning of the list. If you omit the ending index, Python assumes it's the end of the list.

```
# Slicing from the beginning
first_three = my_list[:3] # [10, 20, 30]
# Slicing until the end
last_three = my_list[2:]  # [30, 40, 50]
```

You can also specify a step value to skip elements while slicing.

```
# Slicing with a step of 2
every_second = my_list[::2]  # [10, 30, 50]
```

Negative step values can be used to reverse the order of the sliced list.

```
# Slicing with a negative step to reverse the list
reversed_list = my_list[::-1]  # [50, 40, 30, 20, 10]
```

List indexing and slicing are powerful tools for working with collections of data. They allow you to access and manipulate elements efficiently, whether you're retrieving specific items or creating new lists based on subsets of existing ones.

In Python, you can update the values of a list by assigning new values to specific elements using indexing. Lists are mutable, meaning their elements can be changed after they are created. Here's how you can update list values:

```
my_list = [10, 20, 30, 40, 50]
# Updating a single element
my_list[2] = 35  # Updating the value at index 2 to 35
print(my_list)  # Output: [10, 20, 35, 40, 50]
```

You can also update multiple elements at once using slicing:

```
my_list = [10, 20, 30, 40, 50]
# Updating multiple elements using slicing
my_list[1:4] = [25, 30, 35]  # Updating values at indices 1, 2, and 3
print(my_list)  # Output: [10, 25, 30, 35, 50]
```

The length of the list does not need to be the same when updating multiple elements using slicing. Python will adjust the list size accordingly:

```
my_list = [10, 20, 30, 40, 50]
# Updating with a different number of elements
my_list[1:4] = [15, 25]  # Updating values at indices 1, 2, and 3
print(my_list)  # Output: [10, 15, 25, 50]
```

You can even use slicing to update the entire list or clear it completely:

```
my_list = [10, 20, 30, 40, 50]
# Updating the entire list
my_list[:] = [1, 2, 3]  # Replacing all elements
print(my_list)  # Output: [1, 2, 3]
```

Keep in mind that updating list values using indexing and slicing modifies the existing list in-place. If you assign a new list to the variable, it won't modify the original list but will create a new one instead:

```
my_list = [10, 20, 30, 40, 50]
new_list = my_list  # Both my_list and new_list point to the same list
new_list[2] = 35  # This will also update my_list
print(my_list)  # Output: [10, 20, 35, 40, 50]
print(new_list)  # Output: [10, 20, 35, 40, 50]
```

Updating list values is a crucial part of working with lists, especially when you need to modify, rearrange, or update data in a collection.

6.1.1 Access elements

In Python, you can access individual items in a list using indexing. Lists are zero-indexed, which means the first element has an index of 0, the second element has an index of 1, and so on. You can also use negative indexing to access elements from the end of the list. Here's how you can access list items:

```
# Create a list
fruits = ["apple", "banana", "cherry", "date", "elderberry"]
# Accessing elements using positive indexing
first_fruit = fruits[0]    # "apple"
second_fruit = fruits[1]   # "banana"
third_fruit = fruits[2]    # "cherry"
# Accessing elements using negative indexing
last_fruit = fruits[-1]    # "elderberry"
second_to_last_fruit = fruits[-2]  # "date"
print(first_fruit, second_fruit, third_fruit, last_fruit, second_to_last_fruit)
```

In this example, the list "fruits" contains five elements. Positive indexing is used to access the first, second, and third elements, while negative indexing is used to access the last and second-to-last elements.

It's important to remember that list indices start from 0 and go up to length-1. Attempting to access an index that is out of range will result in an "IndexError."

```
# Accessing an index that is out of range
# This will result in an IndexError
invalid_index = fruits[5]
```

List slicing can also be used to access a range of elements within a list:

```
# Slicing to access a range of elements
selected_fruits = fruits[1:4]  # ["banana", "cherry", "date"]
```

Slicing includes elements from the starting index up to, but not including, the ending index. This can be helpful when you need to work with a subset of the list.

Accessing list items in Python involves using index values to retrieve individual elements. Lists provide a flexible way to store and manipulate collections of data, and understanding how to access their elements is a fundamental skill in programming.

6.1.2 Negative indexing

Negative indexing in Python lists allows you to access elements from the end of the list. When you use negative indices, -1 refers to the last item, -2 refers to the second-to-last item, and so on. This provides a convenient way to access elements without needing to know the exact length of the list.

For example, consider a list **thislist = ["apple", "banana", "cherry"]**. Using negative indexing:

- **thislist[-1]** refers to the last item, which is "cherry".
- **thislist[-2]** refers to the second-to-last item, which is "banana".
- **thislist[-3]** refers to the third-to-last item, which is "apple".

Here's the example code:

```
thislist = ["apple", "banana", "cherry"]
# Accessing elements using negative indexing
last_item = thislist[-1]         # "cherry"
second_to_last_item = thislist[-2]  # "banana"
print("Last item:", last_item)
print("Second-to-last item:", second_to_last_item)
```

Negative indexing is a useful feature in Python that simplifies access to elements at the end of lists without needing to calculate their exact positions based on the list's length.

6.1.3 Add elements

In Python, you can add items to a list using various methods. Lists are dynamic and versatile data structures that allow you to modify their contents easily. Let's explore the different ways to add items to a list in detail:

Using append() Method: The **append()** method is used to add a single element to the end of the list. It modifies the list in-place and is a simple way to extend the list.

```
fruits = ["apple", "banana", "cherry"]
fruits.append("orange")
print(fruits)  # Output: ["apple", "banana", "cherry", "orange"]
```

Using insert() Method: The **insert()** method allows you to add an element at a specific index in the list. Existing elements are shifted to the right.

```
numbers = [1, 2, 3, 5, 6]
numbers.insert(3, 4)  # Inserting 4 at index 3
print(numbers)  # Output: [1, 2, 3, 4, 5, 6]
```

Using Concatenation: You can concatenate two lists using the + operator. This creates a new list containing elements from both lists.

```
list1 = [1, 2, 3]
list2 = [4, 5, 6]
concatenated_list = list1 + list2
print(concatenated_list)  # Output: [1, 2, 3, 4, 5, 6]
list1 = [1, 2, 3]
list2 = [4, 5, 6]
concatenated_list = list1 + list2
print(concatenated_list)  # Output: [1, 2, 3, 4, 5, 6]
```

Using List Slicing: You can use list slicing to add multiple elements to specific positions in the list. This method allows you to replace a range of elements with a new list.

```
data = [10, 20, 30, 40, 50]
data[1:4] = [25, 35, 45]  # Replacing values at indices 1, 2, and 3
print(data)  # Output: [10, 25, 35, 45, 50]
```

Using extend() Method: The **extend()** method is used to append multiple elements from an iterable (another list, tuple, etc.) to the end of the list.

```
vegetables = ["carrot", "lettuce"]
new_vegetables = ["broccoli", "spinach"]
vegetables.extend(new_vegetables)
print(vegetables)  # Output: ["carrot", "lettuce", "broccoli", "spinach"]
```

These are some of the common ways to add items to a list in Python. The choice of method depends on your specific use case and the desired behavior. Lists in Python are dynamic, so you can easily modify their contents and adapt them to your program's requirements.

You can remove items from a list using various methods. Lists are mutable, which means you can modify their contents, including removing elements. Let's explore the different ways to remove items from a list with examples:

Using remove() Method: The **remove()** method is used to remove the first occurrence of a specific value from the list. If the value is not found, it raises a ValueError.

```
fruits = ["apple", "banana", "cherry", "banana"]
fruits.remove("banana")
print(fruits)  # Output: ["apple", "cherry", "banana"]
```

Using pop() Method: The **pop()** method removes an element at a specified index and returns its value. If no index is provided, it removes and returns the last element. This method also allows you to capture the removed value.

```
numbers = [10, 20, 30, 40, 50]
removed_value = numbers.pop(2)  # Remove element at index 2 (30)
print(removed_value)  # Output: 30
print(numbers)  # Output: [10, 20, 40, 50]
```

Using del Statement: The **del** statement is used to delete an element or a slice from the list. It doesn't return the deleted element(s) and modifies the list in-place.

```
colors = ["red", "green", "blue", "yellow"]
del colors[1]  # Delete element at index 1 ("green")
print(colors)  # Output: ["red", "blue", "yellow"]
```

Using clear() Method: The **clear()** method removes all elements from the list, making it empty.

```
pets = ["dog", "cat", "rabbit"]
pets.clear()
print(pets)  # Output: []
```

Using List Comprehension: List comprehension can be used to create a new list by excluding certain elements based on a condition.

```
numbers = [1, 2, 3, 4, 5, 6, 7, 8, 9, 10]
filtered_numbers = [num for num in numbers if num % 2 == 0]  # Remove odd numbers
print(filtered_numbers)  # Output: [2, 4, 6, 8, 10]
```

These are some common methods for removing items from a list in Python. The method you choose depends on the specific behavior you want to achieve. It's important to note that these methods modify the list in-place, so you should be cautious when using them.

6.2 Python Tuple

A tuple in Python is a collection of ordered, immutable elements enclosed in parentheses ( ). Tuples are similar to lists, but the main difference is that tuples are immutable, which means their elements cannot be modified after creation. This immutability can be useful when you want to create a collection of values that should not change during the course of your program.

Here's an explanation of tuples with examples:

Creating Tuples: You can create a tuple by enclosing comma-separated values in parentheses.

```
# Creating a tuple
my_tuple = (1, 2, 3, 4, 5)
print(my_tuple)  # Output: (1, 2, 3, 4, 5)
```

Accessing Elements: You can access elements of a tuple using indexing, just like with lists.

```
# Accessing tuple elements
first_element = my_tuple[0]  # 1
second_element = my_tuple[1]  # 2
```

Tuples with Mixed Data Types: Tuples can contain elements of different data types.

```
mixed_tuple = ("apple", 3.14, 42, True)
```

Tuple Packing and Unpacking: Tuple packing is the process of creating a tuple with comma-separated values. Tuple unpacking involves assigning tuple elements to variables.

```
# Tuple packing
person = ("John", 25, "USA")
# Tuple unpacking
name, age, country = person
print(name, age, country) # Output: John 25 USA
```

Tuples as Return Values: Functions can return multiple values as a tuple, which can then be unpacked.

```
def get_name_age():
return "Alice", 30
name, age = get_name_age()
```

Immutable Nature: Unlike lists, tuples are immutable. Once created, their elements cannot be changed.

```
my_tuple[0] = 10  # This will result in a TypeError
```

Tuples vs. Lists: Tuples are useful when you want to ensure that data remains unchanged. Lists are more flexible and allow modification of elements.

```
my_list = [1, 2, 3]
my_tuple = (1, 2, 3)
my_list[0] = 10  # Valid
my_tuple[0] = 10  # TypeError: 'tuple' object does not support item assignment
```

Tuples are often used when you want to create a collection of items that shouldn't change, like coordinates, configuration settings, or items in a database record. They provide a lightweight alternative to lists for scenarios where immutability is desired.

6.3 Dictionary in Python

A dictionary in Python is an unordered collection of key-value pairs, where each key is unique and maps to a specific value. Dictionaries are also known as "associative arrays" or "hash maps" in other programming languages. They are very useful for storing and retrieving data based on descriptive keys rather than numerical indices, providing efficient and convenient access to information.

Here's an explanation of dictionaries with examples:

Creating Dictionaries: Dictionaries are created using curly braces {}. Each key-value pair is separated by a colon **:** and pairs are separated by commas.

```
# Creating a dictionary
student = {
   "name": "Alice",
   "age": 25,
   "grade": "A",
   "city": "New York"
}
```

Accessing Values: You can access values in a dictionary using their corresponding keys.

```
name = student["name"] # "Alice"
age = student["age"]   # 25
```

Adding and Updating Items: You can add new key-value pairs or update existing values.

```
# Adding a new key-value pair
student["gender"] = "Female"
# Updating a value
student["age"] = 26
```

Dictionary Methods: Dictionaries have various methods for manipulation, such as **keys()**, **values()**, and **items()**, which return views of the keys, values, and key-value pairs respectively.

```
keys = student.keys()   # ["name", "age", "grade", "city", "gender"]
values = student.values() # ["Alice", 26, "A", "New York", "Female"]
items = student.items() # [("name", "Alice"), ("age", 26), ...]
```

Removing Items: You can use the **del** statement to remove a specific key-value pair.

```
del student["grade"]
```

Checking for Key Existence: You can use the **in** keyword to check if a key exists in the dictionary.

```
if "age" in student:
```

```
    print("Age:", student["age"])
```

Nested Dictionaries: Dictionaries can contain other dictionaries as values, allowing for more complex data structures.

```
family = {
    "father": {"name": "John", "age": 45},
    "mother": {"name": "Jane", "age": 40}
}
```

Dictionaries are versatile data structures in Python that allow you to associate values with descriptive keys. They are commonly used for tasks like storing settings, managing databases, and representing real-world objects and relationships.

6.4 Set in Python

A set in Python is an unordered collection of unique elements. Sets are useful when you want to store a collection of items where the order doesn't matter and you want to ensure that each item appears only once. Sets are also commonly used to perform various mathematical operations like union, intersection, and difference.

Here's an explanation of sets with examples:

Creating Sets: Sets are created using curly braces **{}**. Each element is separated by a comma.

```
# Creating a set
fruits = {"apple", "banana", "cherry"}
```

Adding Elements: You can add elements to a set using the **add()** method.

```
fruits.add("orange")
```

Removing Elements: You can remove elements from a set using the **remove()** or **discard()** methods. The **remove()** method raises an error if the element doesn't exist, while **discard()** does not.

```
fruits.remove("banana")
fruits.discard("pear")
```

Set Operations: Sets support mathematical operations like union, intersection, and difference.

```
set1 = {1, 2, 3, 4}
set2 = {3, 4, 5, 6}
union = set1 | set2        # {1, 2, 3, 4, 5, 6}
intersection = set1 & set2  # {3, 4}
difference = set1 - set2   # {1, 2}
```

Checking Membership: You can use the **in** keyword to check if an element is in the set.

```
if "apple" in fruits:
print("An apple is in the set")
```

Iterating Over Sets: You can use a **for** loop to iterate over the elements of a set.

```
for fruit in fruits:
    print(fruit)
```

Set Comprehensions: You can create sets using comprehensions, similar to list comprehensions.

```
even_numbers = {x for x in range(10) if x % 2 == 0}
```

Sets are particularly useful when you want to work with collections of unique elements and perform set-related operations efficiently. They are a versatile data structure that can simplify tasks involving distinct values and membership testing.

6.5 del statement in Python

In Python, the del statement is used to delete or remove objects from memory. It can be used to remove variables, elements from a list, slices from a list, attributes from an object, and more. The del statement is a powerful tool for managing memory and resources in your program.

Here are some common uses of the del statement:

Deleting Variables: You can use the del statement to remove a variable and its associated data from memory.

```
x = 10
del x  # Deletes the variable 'x'
```

Deleting List Elements: You can use the **del** statement to remove specific elements from a list.

```
numbers = [1, 2, 3, 4, 5]
del numbers[2]  # Removes the element at index 2 (3)
```

Deleting Slices from a List: You can also use the **del** statement to remove a range of elements from a list using slicing

```
numbers = [1, 2, 3, 4, 5]
del numbers[1:4]  # Removes elements at indices 1, 2, and 3
```

Deleting Attributes: You can use the **del** statement to delete attributes from objects.

```
class Person:
```

```
    def __init__(self, name):
        self.name = name
person = Person("Alice")
del person.name  # Deletes the 'name' attribute
```

Deleting Entire Objects: You can use the **del** statement to delete an entire object, which releases its memory and resources.

```
my_dict = {"a": 1, "b": 2, "c": 3}
del my_dict["b"]  # Removes the key-value pair with key "b"
```

Summary

Lists: Lists are ordered collections of items, which can be of different types. They are mutable, meaning you can modify their elements after creation. Lists are created using square brackets and can store duplicate values.

Tuples: Tuples are similar to lists but are immutable, meaning their elements cannot be changed after creation. They are created using parentheses and are often used for grouping related data.

Sets: Sets are unordered collections of unique elements. They are useful for storing and manipulating distinct values. Sets are created using curly braces and can perform set operations like union, intersection, and difference.

Dictionaries: Dictionaries are collections of key-value pairs. They provide a way to associate values with unique keys, making it easy to look up values based on their keys. Dictionaries are created using curly braces and colons to separate keys and values.

Strings: Strings are sequences of characters and are used to represent textual data. They are immutable, so you cannot change individual characters within a string. Python offers various string manipulation methods for working with text.

Lists, Tuples, and Dictionaries Comprehensions: Comprehensions provide a concise way to create lists, tuples, and dictionaries by applying an expression to each item in an iterable. They offer a more readable and efficient alternative to traditional loops.

Sets and Maps (Using the set and collections module): The **set** data structure in Python provides an implementation of sets, while the **collections** module offers specialized data structures like defaultdict, Counter, and OrderedDict for various advanced use cases.

These data structures serve as essential building blocks in Python programming, allowing you to handle a wide range of data organization and manipulation tasks effectively.

Exercise 1:
Multiple Choice Questions (MCQs):

Question 1: Which Python data structure is ordered, mutable, and allows duplicate elements?
a) List
b) Tuple
c) Set
d) Dictionary

Question 2: In a Python dictionary, what is the purpose of the keys?
a) To store values
b) To maintain order
c) To allow duplicate entries
d) To uniquely identify values

Question 3: Which data structure follows the Last-In-First-Out (LIFO) principle?
a) Queue
b) Set
c) Stack
d) Tuple

Question 4: Which of the following is not a built-in data structure in Python?
a) Array
b) List
c) Tuple
d) Dictionary

Question 5: Which Python data structure is used to store unique elements and supports set operations like union and intersection?
a) List
b) Tuple
c) Set
d) Dictionary
Question 6: Which data structure is used to implement a circular buffer efficiently?
a) Stack
b) Queue
c) Linked List
d) Set
Question 7: What is the key characteristic of an immutable data structure?
a) It can change its size dynamically.
b) It can have duplicate elements.
c) Its elements cannot be modified after creation.
d) It is not suitable for storing textual data.
Question 8: Which module in Python provides advanced data structures like defaultdict and OrderedDict?
a) collections
b) array
c) numpy
d) math
Answer
1. a 2. d 3. c 4. a 5. c 6. b 7. c 8. A

Exercise 2:
True/False Questions:
Question 1: Lists in Python are immutable.
Question 2: Tuples allow for elements to be changed after creation.
Question 3: Dictionaries in Python store data in a structured, ordered manner.
Question 4: Python dictionaries maintain the order of elements based on insertion.
Question 5: A queue follows the Last-In-First-Out (LIFO) principle.
Answer
1. False 2. False 3. False 4. True 5. False

Exercise 3:
Review questions:
Question 1: What are the primary data structures available in Python for storing collections of items?
Question 2: How do lists and tuples differ in terms of mutability?
Question 3: What is the primary use case for dictionaries in Python?
Question 4: How do you initialize an empty set?
Question 5: Can a list contain another list as an element?
Question 6: What is the difference between **append()** and **extend()** methods in a list?
Question 7: How do you access the values in a dictionary?
Question 8: What is the purpose of the **zip()** function when working with lists and tuples?
Question 9: How do you remove an element from a set?
Question 10: What types of keys are allowed in a Python dictionary?
Question 11: Can a tuple contain mutable elements, like a list?
Question 12: How would you create a list with repeated elements?
Question 13: What is list comprehension and how is it useful?
Question 14: How do you sort the elements in a list?
Question 15: What are the key methods to add or remove elements in a dictionary?
Question 16: How do you convert a list into a tuple and vice versa?
Question 17: How do you check if an element exists in a list or tuple without using a loop?
Question 18: What is the role of the **enumerate()** function when working with lists?
Question 19: How do you merge two dictionaries?
Question 20: What are some ways to iterate through all elements in a list and a dictionary?

Chapter 7

Python condition Statement (if-else)

Conditional statements in Python allow you to make decisions in your code based on conditions. These statements enable your program to execute different code blocks depending on whether a certain condition is true or false. The most common types of conditional statements in Python are the **if**, **elif** (short for "else if"), and **else** statements. Let's explore each of them:

Statement	Description
If Statement	The if statement is used to test a specific condition. If the condition is true, a block of code (if-block) will be executed.
If - else Statement	The if-else statement is similar to if statement except the fact that, it also provides the block of the code for the false case of the condition to be checked. If the condition provided in the if statement is false, then the else statement will be executed.
Nested if Statement	Nested if statements enable us to use if ? else statement inside an outer if statement.

In Python, conditional statements act as the decision-making mechanisms, enabling you to direct the flow of your program based on specific conditions. These statements help to evaluate whether a particular condition is true or false, subsequently executing code blocks accordingly. The most prevalent conditional statements are if, elif (an abbreviation for "else if"), and else, each serving a unique role in conditional logic.

The if statement assesses a given condition; if the condition is true, the subsequent code block is executed. This is the most basic form of conditional programming, allowing you to set up a single condition for evaluation.

On the other hand, if-else statements bring an additional layer of functionality. While the if portion tests a condition, the else part provides an alternative code block that will execute if the condition fails. This structure allows your program to have a 'fallback' plan when a specific condition is not met.

Moreover, Python allows for more complex decision-making through nested if statements and the elif keyword. Nested if statements mean you can place an if statement within another, offering multiple layers of conditions. The elif statement is used to chain multiple conditions sequentially. This is particularly useful when you have more than two possible outcomes for a single evaluation.

Overall, conditional statements in Python give your programs the capability to respond differently to various inputs or states. They add flexibility and sophistication to your code, enabling it to adapt and react according to the conditions it encounters.

7.1 The if statement

if Statement: The **if** statement is a fundamental control structure in Python that allows you to execute a block of code only if a specified condition evaluates to **True**. It's used to introduce decision-making into your programs, allowing them to respond differently based on the current state or inputs.

Here's a more detailed explanation of the **if** statement along with examples:

Syntax: if condition:

```
    # Code to execute if the condition is True
```

The **condition** is an expression that is evaluated to either **True** or **False**.

If the **condition** is **True**, the code block indented under the **if** statement is executed.

If the **condition** is **False**, the indented code block is skipped, and the program continues with the next statement after the **if** block.

```
x = 10
if x > 5:
    print("x is greater than 5")
```

In this example, the condition **x > 5** evaluates to **True** because **x** is indeed greater than 5. Therefore, the code inside the indented block (**print("x is greater than 5")**) is executed, and the output is "x is greater than 5".

Another example:

```
x = 19
if x > 5:
    print("x is greater than 5")
```

7.2 Using if-else:

The **if-else** statement in Python allows you to execute different blocks of code based on whether a condition is **True** or **False**. This construct is useful when you want to provide alternative actions for cases where the initial condition isn't met. Here's how the **if-else** statement works, along with an example:

Syntax:

```
if condition:
    # Code to execute if the condition is True
else:
    # Code to execute if the condition is False
```

- If the **condition** is **True**, the code block indented under the **if** statement is executed, and the code block under the **else** statement is skipped.
- If the **condition** is **False**, the code block indented under the **else** statement is executed, and the code block under the **if** statement is skipped.

```
x = 7
if x > 10:
    print("x is greater than 10")
else:
    print("x is not greater than 10")
```

In this example, **x** is 7, which is not greater than 10. So, the condition **x > 10** is **False**, and the code block under the **else** statement is executed. The output will be "x is not greater than 10".

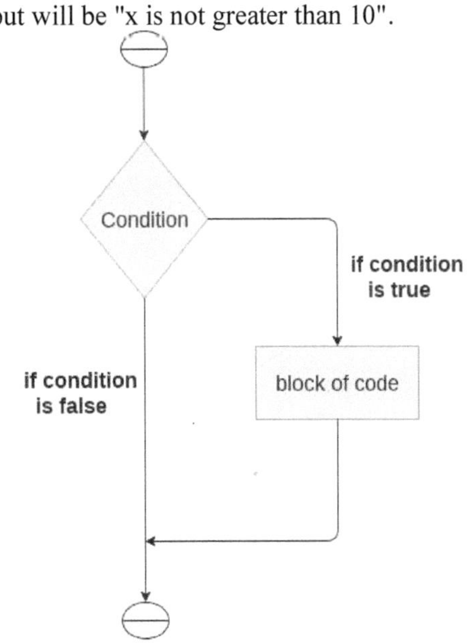

7.3 Nested if-else Statements

You can also nest **if-else** statements to handle more complex scenarios.

```
x = 12
if x > 5:
    if x < 10:
        print("x is between 5 and 10")
    else:
        print("x is greater than or equal to 10")
else:
    print("x is 5 or less")
```

In this example, the outer **if** condition checks whether **x** is greater than 5. Since **x** is indeed greater than 5, the program enters the nested block. The nested **if** condition checks whether **x** is less than 10. Since this condition is **False** (because **x** is 12), the program executes the **else** block inside the nested **if-else**. As a result, the output will be "x is greater than or equal to 10".

The **if-else** statement provides a way to choose between two different courses of action based on a condition's truth value. It's a fundamental construct for controlling program flow and making decisions in your code.

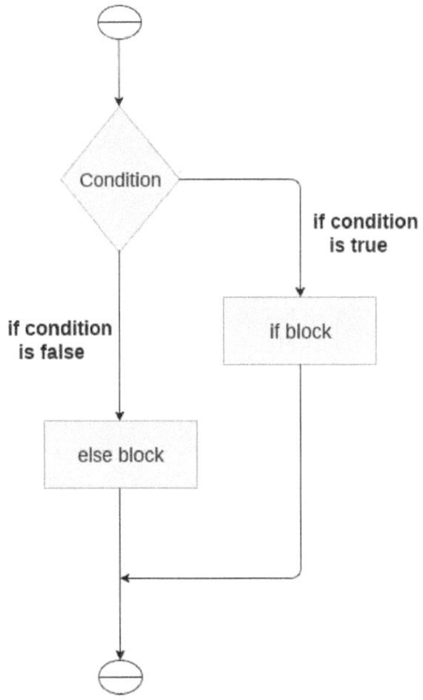

7.4 if-elif-else statement

The **if-elif-else** statement in Python is used when you have multiple conditions to check. It allows you to specify multiple conditions and their corresponding code blocks. This construct is useful when you want to create a decision tree with several possible outcomes. Here's how the **if-elif-else** statement works, along with an example:

```
if condition1:
    # Code to execute if condition1 is True
elif condition2:
    # Code to execute if condition2 is True
elif condition3:
    # Code to execute if condition3 is True
else:
    # Code to execute if none of the conditions are True
```

The **if** condition is evaluated first. If it's **True**, the corresponding code block is executed, and the rest of the **elif** and **else** blocks are skipped.

If the **if** condition is **False**, the program evaluates the **elif** conditions sequentially, executing the first code block where the condition is **True**.

If none of the conditions (including the **if** and all **elif** conditions) are **True**, the code block under the **else** statement is executed.

```
x = 7
if x > 10:
    print("x is greater than 10")
elif x > 5:
    print("x is greater than 5 but not greater than 10")
else:
    print("x is 5 or less")
```

In this example, **x** is 7. The first condition **x > 10** is **False**, so the program checks the next condition. The second condition **x > 5** is **True**, and the corresponding code block is executed. Therefore, the output will be "x is greater than 5 but not greater than 10".

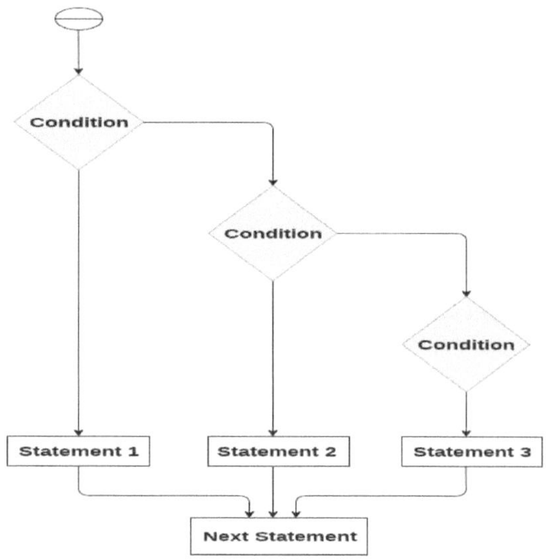

7.5 Nested if-elif-else Statements

You can also nest **if-elif-else** statements to handle more complex scenarios with multiple layers of decision-making.

```
x = 12
if x > 5:
   if x < 10:
      print("x is between 5 and 10")
   else:
      print("x is greater than or equal to 10")
else:
   print("x is 5 or less")
```

In this example, the outer **if** condition checks whether **x** is greater than 5. Since **x** is indeed greater than 5, the program enters the nested block. The nested **if** condition checks whether **x** is less than 10. Since this condition is **False** (because **x** is 12), the program executes the **else** block inside the nested **if-else**. As a result, the output will be "x is greater than or equal to 10".The **if-elif-else** statement is a versatile construct that allows you to handle complex decision trees in your programs, providing different paths of execution based on various conditions.

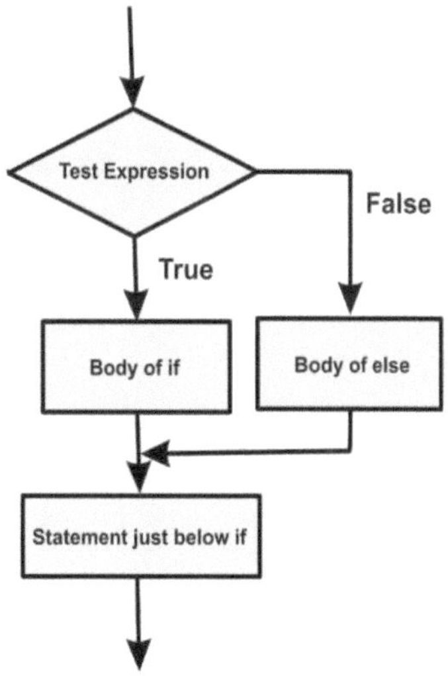

7.6 Nested if Statements

You can also nest conditional statements within each other to handle more complex situations.

A nested **if** statement in Python is when one **if** statement is placed inside another **if** statement. This allows you to create more complex decision-making structures by checking multiple conditions and executing different blocks of code based on those conditions. Nested **if** statements are especially useful when you need to handle various levels of decision-making.

Here's a more detailed explanation of nested **if** statements along with an example:

```
if outer_condition:
    # Code for outer condition
    if inner_condition:
        # Code for inner condition
    else:
        # Code if inner_condition is False
else:
    # Code if outer_condition is False
```

The outer **if** statement evaluates the **outer_condition**. If it's **True**, the code block indented under the outer **if** statement is executed. If it's **False**, the program skips the outer code block and continues with the next statement.

If the **inner_condition** (inside the inner **if** statement) is **True**, the code block indented under the inner **if** statement is executed. If it's **False**, the program skips the inner code block and either executes the **else** block or continues with the next statement after the nested **if** statement.

```
x = 12
if x > 5:
    print("x is greater than 5")
    if x < 10:
        print("x is also less than 10")
    else:
        print("x is greater than or equal to 10")
else:
    print("x is 5 or less")
```

In this example, the outer **if** condition checks whether **x** is greater than 5. Since **x** is indeed greater than 5, the code block under the outer **if** is executed. Inside the outer **if** block, there's a nested **if** condition that checks whether **x** is less than 10. Since **x** is 12, the inner condition is **False**, and the code block under the **else** statement within the nested **if** is executed. Therefore, the output will be:

```
x is greater than 5
x is greater than or equal to 10
```

Nested **if** statements provide a way to add additional layers of decision-making to your code, allowing you to handle more complex scenarios where multiple conditions need to be evaluated. However, it's important to keep your code organized and readable when using nested **if** statements, as excessive nesting can make your code harder to understand and maintain.

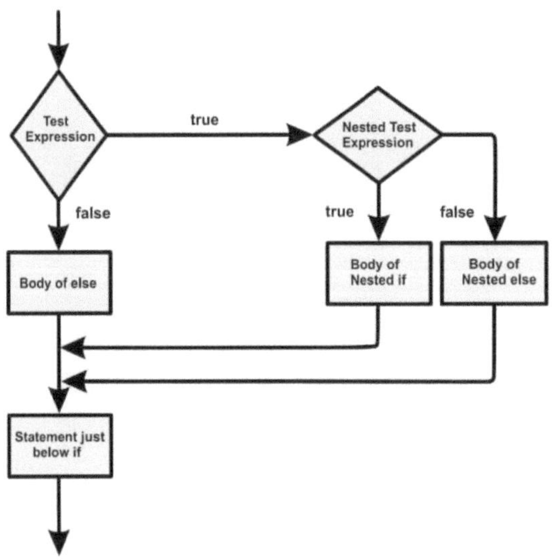

7.7 Short hand if statement

In Python, the shorthand if statement, also known as the ternary conditional operator, allows you to test a condition and return a value based on the result of that condition in a single line.

The syntax is:

```
value_if_true if condition else value_if_false
```

This is a more concise way to write an **if-else** statement, and it's often used for simple conditional assignments.

Example:

Let's say you want to assign a variable **x** the value **'Even'** if another variable **num** is even, and **'Odd'** otherwise. Using the shorthand **if** statement, you could write:

```
num = 10  # some integer value
x = 'Even' if num % 2 == 0 else 'Odd'
```

In this example, **num % 2 == 0** is the condition being checked. If it's **True**, **x** will be assigned the value **'Even'**. If it's **False**, **x** will be assigned the value **'Odd'**.

Another Example:

Suppose you have two variables **a** and **b**, and you want to find the minimum of these two variables and assign it to a variable called **minimum**.

Here's how you could do it with a shorthand **if** statement:

```
a = 5
b = 10
minimum = a if a < b else b
```

If **a** is less than **b**, then **minimum** will be assigned the value of **a**. Otherwise, **minimum** will be assigned the value of **b**.

While shorthand **if** statements make your code more concise, they can also make it less readable if the condition being checked is complex or if you're nesting multiple ternary operators. In such cases, it's often better to stick with the traditional **if-else** statements for the sake of clarity.

7.8 Short hand if..else statement

In Python, the shorthand if ... else statement, commonly known as the ternary conditional operator, lets you execute an if-else condition in a single, more concise line. This is particularly useful for simple conditional checks.

Syntax

The syntax of the shorthand if ... else statement in Python is:

```
result = value_if_true if condition else value_if_false
```

Here, condition is evaluated first. If it's True, then result is assigned **value_if_true**. If it's **False**, then **result** is assigned value_if_false.

Example 1: Simple Condition

Let's say you want to determine if a number is even or odd. Normally, you'd use an **if-else** statement like this:

```
num = 10  # An example number

if num % 2 == 0:
    result = "Even"
else:
    result = "Odd"
```

Using the shorthand if ... else statement, you can achieve the same result in a single line:

```
num = 10  # An example number
result = "Even" if num % 2 == 0 else "Odd"
```

Example 2: Finding the Minimum Value

In another example, consider you have two numbers, a and b, and you want to find the minimum of the two.

Traditional if-else approach:

```
a = 5
b = 10

if a < b:
    minimum = a
else:
```

```
    minimum = b
```

Using shorthand if ... else:

```
a = 5
b = 10
minimum = a if a < b else b
```

Readability Considerations

Although the shorthand if ... else can make your code more concise, it's important to use it judiciously. For complex conditions or multiple nested conditions, the shorthand syntax can become hard to read and understand. In such cases, it's often better to use the standard if-else statements for clarity.

Shorthand if ... else is a more compact way to execute if-else conditions in Python, but it's best suited for simple conditions to maintain readability.

7.9 AND OR NOT statements

In Python, you can use the logical operators and, or, and not along with if and else statements to create more complex conditional logic. These operators are:

- and: Returns True if both the conditions are true
- or: Returns True if at least one condition is true
- not: Returns True if the condition is false

Using and in if Statements

The and operator is used when you want multiple conditions to be true.

```
x = 10
y = 5

if x > 5 and y > 1:
    print("Both conditions are True")
else:
    print("At least one condition is False")
```

Using or in if Statements

The **or** operator is used when at least one condition needs to be true.

```
x = 2
y = 5

if x > 5 or y > 1:
    print("At least one condition is True")
else:
    print("Both conditions are False")
```

Using not in if Statements

The **not** operator is used to invert a condition.

```
x = 10

if not x < 5:
    print("x is not less than 5")
else:
    print("x is less than 5")
```

Combining and, or, not

You can combine these logical operators for more complex conditions.

```
x = 10
y = 5
z = -1

if x > 5 and (y > 1 or not z > 0):
    print("The complex condition is True")
```

```
else:
    print("The complex condition is False")
```

In this example, the condition x > 5 and (y > 1 or not z > 0) will evaluate to True because:

x > 5 is True

y > 1 or not z > 0 is True because y > 1 is True

As both are True, the and operator returns True, and thus the if block is executed.

Understanding the precedence and associativity of these logical operators (not is evaluated first, followed by and, and then or) can help you effectively combine them in complex conditions. Use parentheses to explicitly specify the order of evaluation when necessary.

Summary

Purpose: Conditional statements allow for decision-making in Python programs by executing different code blocks based on specific conditions.

if Statement: Executes a block of code only if a given condition is true.

if-else Statement: Provides an alternative code block to execute when the condition in the "if" statement is false.

if-elif-else Statement: Handles multiple conditions in sequence, executing the block associated with the first true condition encountered.

Nested if Statements: Allows placing one or more conditional statements within another, enabling complex decision structures.

Conditions: Are expressions that evaluate to either true or false, using comparison operators like "==", "!=", "<", ">", "<=", ">=", and logical operators "and", "or", "not".

Flow Control: Conditional statements are vital for directing program flow, enabling dynamic behaviors based on different situations.

Exercise 1:

Multiple Choice Questions (MCQs):

Question 1: What is the primary purpose of conditional statements in Python?

a) To repeat code blocks
b) To create functions
c) To make decisions and execute code based on conditions
d) To handle exceptions

Question 2: Which statement is used to execute a block of code only if a specified condition is true?

a) if-else
b) if
c) for
d) while

Question 3: Which Python logical operator combines two conditions and evaluates as true only if both conditions are true?

a) and
b) or
c) not
d) xor

Question 4: What is the purpose of the "else" part in an "if-else" statement?

a) It provides an alternative block of code to execute when the "if" condition is true.
b) It executes when the "if" condition is true.
c) It executes when the "if" condition is false.
d) It handles multiple conditions.

Question 5: Which statement is used to handle multiple conditions and execute the block associated with the first true condition?

a) if-else
b) if

c) if-elif-else
d) elif
Question 6: What is the result of the expression **10 > 5 and 7 < 3**?
a) True
b) False
c) Error
d) None
Question 7: Which type of operator is used to compare whether two values are equal?
a) Assignment operator (=)
b) Equality operator (==)
c) Comparison operator (>)
d) Logical operator (and)
Question 8: In nested if statements, what purpose does the inner if statement serve?
a) It executes regardless of the outer condition.
b) It creates confusion and should be avoided.
c) It adds an extra layer of complexity to the code.
d) It allows for additional checks based on the outcome of the outer condition.
Answer
1. c 2. b 3. a 4. c 5. c 6. b 7. b 8. d

Exercise 2:
True or False Statements:
1. True or False: Conditional statements are used to execute different code blocks based on specific conditions.
2. True or False: The "if" statement in Python executes a block of code only if a specified condition is false.
3. True or False: The "if-else" statement is used to handle multiple conditions and execute the block associated with the first true condition.
4. True or False: Conditions in Python evaluate to either true or false, and logical operators like "and", "or", and "not" can be used to combine conditions.
5. True or False: Nested if statements allow placing one or more conditional statements within another to create complex decision structures.

Answer
1. True 2. False 3. False 4. True 5. True

Exercise 3:
Review questions:
Question 1: What is the primary purpose of conditional statements in Python?
Question 2: Can you explain the basic syntax of an **if** statement?
Question 3: How does the **elif** keyword extend the functionality of an **if** statement?
Question 4: What role does the **else** keyword play in conditional statements?
Question 5: Can you nest **if** statements within each other? What is the advantage or disadvantage of doing so?
Question 6: How does Python interpret a zero value in a condition?
Question 7: What types of data can be evaluated as **True** or **False** in a condition?
Question 8: What is short-circuit evaluation in the context of **and** and **or** operators?
Question 9: How is the **not** operator used in conditional statements?
Question 10: Can you compare two strings using conditional operators? If so, how does Python evaluate the condition?
Question 11: How do you check for multiple conditions in a single **if** statement?
Question 12: What is the significance of indentation in Python conditional statements?
Question 13: Is it necessary to use the **elif** and **else** clauses with every **if** statement?
Question 14: How do you use the **in** keyword in a condition to check for an item in a list or tuple?
Question 15: Can you use logical operators (**and**, **or**, **not**) in an **if** condition?
Question 16: How would you write a condition to check if a variable is neither **None** nor empty?
Question 17: Can you use conditional statements within list comprehensions?

Question 18: What are ternary conditional operators, and how do they simplify **if-else** statements?
Question 19: How do you test if a dictionary key exists within an **if** statement?
Question 20: How do conditional statements interact with loops like **for** and **while**?

Chapter 8

Function and loops

Loops in Python are programming constructs that allow you to repeat a block of code multiple times. They are used to automate repetitive tasks, iterate over sequences (like lists or strings), and perform actions until a certain condition is met.

In Python, loops and functions are fundamental constructs that enable more efficient and reusable code. A loop allows for the repetition of an action or sequence of actions. The two primary types of loops in Python are for loops and while loops. A for loop iterates over an inerrable like a list or a string, executing a block of code for each element. A while loop continues execution as long as a certain condition remains true.

Functions, on the other hand, are reusable pieces of code that perform specific tasks. Defined using the def keyword, functions can take inputs (arguments) and return outputs. They are essential for modular programming and code organization.

Combining loops and functions can be powerful. For instance, a function can include a loop to perform a repetitive calculation or action. Likewise, a loop can call a function multiple times with different arguments, thereby reducing code duplication.

Python has two main types of loops: "for loops" and "while loops.". In Python, there is no C style for loop, i.e., for (i=0; i <n; i++). There is a **"for" loop** which is similar to each loop in other languages. Let us learn how to use a loop for sequential traversals.

8.1 For Loops

A "for loop" in Python is used to iterate over a sequence (such as a list, tuple, string, or range) and perform a set of actions for each element in the sequence. The loop iterates through each item in the sequence and executes a block of code for each iteration.

Here's the basic syntax of a for loop in Python:

```
for element in sequence:
   # code to be executed for each element
```

element: A variable that will take on the value of each item in the sequence during each iteration.

sequence: The sequence of items you want to iterate over.

The indented block of code following the colon is what will be executed for each element in the sequence.

Here's an example of using a for loop to iterate over a list of numbers and print each number:

```
numbers = [1, 2, 3, 4, 5]
for num in numbers:
   print(num)
```

Output:

```
1
2
3
4
5
```

In this example, the loop iterates through each element (number) in the numbers list and prints it.

You can also use the range() function to generate a sequence of numbers to iterate over. Here's an example:

```
for i in range(1, 6):
   print(i)
```

Output:

```
1
2
3
4
5
```

In this example, the **range(1, 6)** generates numbers from 1 to 5 (inclusive) and the loop iterates over these numbers, printing each one.

For loops can be used for a wide variety of tasks, such as processing elements in a container, performing calculations, and more. Just remember that the indentation is crucial in Python, as it defines the scope of the loop's body.

8.1.1 range() function in python

The range() function in Python is used to generate a sequence of numbers. It's commonly used with loops, especially for loops, to iterate over a specific range of values. The range() function returns an immutable sequence type that represents a range of integers. It's important to note that the range() function itself does not create a list of numbers; rather, it generates numbers on-the-fly as needed.

Here's the syntax of the range() function:

```
range(start, stop, step)
```

- **start**: The starting value of the range (inclusive). If omitted, it defaults to 0.
- **stop**: The stopping value of the range (exclusive). The sequence will generate values up to, but not including, this value.
- **step**: The difference between consecutive numbers in the sequence. If omitted, it defaults to 1.

Now, let's look at some examples to understand how the **range()** function works:

Example 1: Generating a sequence of numbers from 0 to 4 (exclusive of 4).

```
for num in range(5):
    print(num)
```

Output:

```
0
1
2
3
```

Example 2: Generating a sequence of even numbers from 0 to 10 (exclusive of 10).

```
for num in range(0, 10, 2):
    print(num)
```

Output:

```
0
2
4
6
8
```

Example 3: Using a range() in a for loop to calculate the sum of numbers from 1 to 10.

```
total = 0
for num in range(1, 11):
    total += num
print(total)
```

Output:

```
55
```

The **range()** function is memory-efficient since it doesn't generate the entire sequence of numbers at once. Instead, it generates the numbers on-the-fly as you iterate over them. This makes it particularly useful for iterating through large ranges without consuming excessive memory.

Keep in mind that if you need an actual list of numbers, you can convert the **range()** to a list using the **list()** function:

```
number_list = list(range(1, 6))
print(number_list)  # Output: [1, 2, 3, 4, 5]
```

Overall, the **range()** function is a versatile tool for generating sequences of numbers, especially when used in conjunction with loops.

8.1.2 Using else statement with for loop

In Python, you can use the else statement with a for loop to specify a block of code that should be executed after the loop completes normally (i.e., not interrupted by a break statement). The code inside the else block will be executed if the loop runs through all iterations without encountering a break statement. This can be useful when you want to perform some action only if a condition is not met during the loop iterations.

Here's the syntax of a for loop with an else statement:

```
for variable in sequence:
    # Loop body
else:
    # Code to execute if the loop completes normally
```

Now, let's look at a couple of examples to illustrate the usage of the **else** statement with a **for** loop:

Example 1: Checking if a number is prime using a **for** loop with an **else** block.

```
num = 17
for i in range(2, int(num ** 0.5) + 1):
    if num % i == 0:
        print(num, "is not prime")
        break
else:
    print(num, "is prime")
```

Output:
17 is prime

In this example, the loop iterates through numbers from 2 to the square root of **num**, checking if any of them divide **num** evenly. If a divisor is found, the loop breaks and the **else** block is not executed. If the loop completes without finding a divisor, the **else** block is executed, indicating that the number is prime.

Example 2: Finding an element in a list using a **for** loop with an **else** block.

```
my_list = [1, 2, 3, 4, 5]
search_value = 6
for item in my_list:
    if item == search_value:
        print("Found", search_value)
        break
else:
    print(search_value, "not found in the list")
```

Output:
6 not found in the list

In this example, the loop iterates through the items in **my_list** and searches for **search_value**. If the value is found, the loop breaks and the **else** block is not executed. If the loop completes without finding the value, the **else** block is executed, indicating that the value is not present in the list.

The **else** statement with a **for** loop can be a powerful tool to handle scenarios where you want to perform an action only if a certain condition is not met during the loop's iterations.

8.1.3 Break statement

The break statement is a control flow statement in Python that is used to immediately exit the innermost loop (either a for loop or a while loop) when a certain condition is met. It's typically used to terminate a loop prematurely when you've achieved a specific goal or condition, allowing you to exit the loop early without completing all iterations.

Here's the syntax of the **break** statement:

```
for variable in sequence:
    if condition:
        # Some code
        break  # Exit the loop immediately
```

Now, let's look at a couple of examples to illustrate the use of the **break** statement:

Example 1: Using **break** to find the first even number in a list.

```
numbers = [3, 5, 8, 11, 12, 15]
for num in numbers:
    if num % 2 == 0:
        print("First even number found:", num)
        break
```

Output:
First even number found: 8

In this example, the loop iterates through the **numbers** list and checks if each number is even. Once an even number is found, the **break** statement is encountered, causing the loop to terminate immediately and the program to print the found even number.

Example 2: Using **break** to search for a specific name in a list.

```
names = ["Alice", "Bob", "Charlie", "David", "Eve"]
search_name = "Charlie"
for name in names:
    if name == search_name:
        print(search_name, "found in the list.")
        break
```

```
else:
    print(search_name, "not found in the list.")
```

Charlie found in the list.

In this example, the loop iterates through the **names** list and compares each name with the **search_name**. If the **search_name** is found, the loop breaks, and the program prints a message indicating that the name is found. If the loop completes without finding the name, the **else** block is executed, indicating that the name is not present in the list.

The **break** statement is useful when you need to stop a loop's execution prematurely based on a certain condition. However, it's important to use it carefully to avoid unexpected behavior, such as accidentally skipping necessary iterations or causing unintended logic errors.

8.1.4 Continue statement

The continue statement is a control flow statement in Python that is used to skip the remaining code inside the current iteration of a loop (either a for loop or a while loop) and move on to the next iteration. It's typically used when you want to skip certain iterations based on a specific condition, without terminating the loop altogether. The loop continues with the next iteration, bypassing any code that follows the continue statement within the current iteration.

Here's the syntax of the continue statement:

```
for variable in sequence:
    if condition:
        # Some code
        continue  # Skip the remaining code in this iteration and move to the next iteration
```

Now, let's look at a couple of examples to illustrate the use of the **continue** statement:

Example 1: Skipping odd numbers in a list.

```
numbers = [1, 2, 3, 4, 5, 6, 7, 8, 9, 10]
for num in numbers:
    if num % 2 != 0:
        continue
    print("Even number:", num)
```

Output:

```
Even number: 2
Even number: 4
Even number: 6
Even number: 8
Even number: 10
```

In this example, the loop iterates through the **numbers** list. When an odd number is encountered, the **continue** statement is triggered, skipping the remaining code in that iteration (the **print** statement) and moving on to the next iteration.

```
names = ["Alice", "Bob", "Charlie", "David", "Eve"]
names_to_skip = ["Bob", "Eve"]
for name in names:
    if name in names_to_skip:
        continue
    print("Processing:", name)
```

Output:

```
Processing: Alice
Processing: Charlie
Processing: David
```

In this example, the loop iterates through the **names** list. When a name that is in the **names_to_skip** list is encountered, the **continue** statement is triggered, skipping the processing of that name and moving on to the next name.

The **continue** statement can be useful when you need to selectively skip certain iterations based on specific conditions. However, it's important to use it judiciously to ensure that your loop logic remains clear and easy to understand, as excessive use of **continue** statements can sometimes make code more complex and harder to maintain.

8.1.5 Else in for loop

In a for loop in Python, you can use the else statement to specify a block of code that should be executed after the loop completes normally (i.e., without being interrupted by a break statement). The else block will not be executed if the loop is terminated by a break statement. This can be useful when you want to perform some action only if the loop completes all iterations without encountering a specific condition.

Here's the syntax of using else with a for loop:

```
for variable in sequence:
    # Loop body
else:
    # Code to execute if the loop completes normally (without a break)
```

Now, let's look at an example to illustrate the usage of the **else** statement with a **for** loop:

Example: Checking for prime numbers using a **for** loop with an **else** block.

```
for num in range(10, 20):
    for i in range(2, int(num ** 0.5) + 1):
        if num % i == 0:
            print(num, "is not prime")
            break
    else:
        print(num, "is prime")
```

Output :

```
10 is not prime
11 is prime
12 is not prime
13 is prime
14 is not prime
15 is not prime
16 is not prime
17 is prime
18 is not prime
19 is prime
```

Here's another example using the **else** statement with a **for** loop:

Example: Searching for an element in a list using a **for** loop with an **else** block.

```
fruits = ["apple", "banana", "orange", "grape", "pear"]
search_fruit = "grapefruit"
for fruit in fruits:
    if fruit == search_fruit:
        print(search_fruit, "found in the list.")
        break
else:
    print(search_fruit, "not found in the list.")
```

Output :

```
grapefruit not found in the list.
```

In this example, the loop iterates through the **fruits** list and compares each fruit with the **search_fruit**. If the **search_fruit** is found, the loop is terminated using **break**, and the **else** block is not executed. If the loop completes without finding the fruit, the **else** block is executed, indicating that the fruit is not present in the list.

8.1.6 Nested Loop

This pattern can be useful for scenarios where you want to take specific action if a particular condition is not met during the loop's iterations. The **else** statement provides a way to handle the case when the loop completes all iterations without encountering a condition that requires early termination. A nested loop in Python is a loop within another loop. It allows you to iterate over a sequence using one loop (the outer loop) and, for each iteration of the outer loop, iterate over another sequence using a separate loop (the inner loop). Nested loops are useful for working with 2D data structures, such as matrices, grids, and tables, where you need to access each element by row and column.

Here's the basic syntax of a nested loop:

```
for outer_item in outer_sequence:
    # Outer loop code
    for inner_item in inner_sequence:
        # Inner loop code
```

- **outer_item**: A variable that iterates over the outer sequence.
- **outer_sequence**: The sequence you want to iterate over with the outer loop.
- **inner_item**: A variable that iterates over the inner sequence.
- **inner_sequence**: The sequence you want to iterate over with the inner loop.

Now, let's go through an example to understand nested loops better:
Example: Printing a multiplication table using nested loops.

```
for i in range(1, 6):  # Outer loop for rows
    for j in range(1, 11):  # Inner loop for columns
        product = i * j
        print(f"{i} * {j} = {product}")
    print()  # Print an empty line after each row
```

Output:

```
1 * 1 = 1
1 * 2 = 2
1 * 3 = 3
1 * 4 = 4
1 * 5 = 5
1 * 6 = 6
1 * 7 = 7
1 * 8 = 8
1 * 9 = 9
1 * 10 = 10

2 * 1 = 2
2 * 2 = 4
2 * 3 = 6
2 * 4 = 8
2 * 5 = 10
2 * 6 = 12
2 * 7 = 14
2 * 8 = 16
2 * 9 = 18
2 * 10 = 20
```

... (and so on for the other rows)

In this example, the outer loop iterates over numbers from 1 to 5, representing the rows of the multiplication table. For each row, the inner loop iterates over numbers from 1 to 10, representing the columns. The product of the row and column is calculated and printed, and an empty line is printed after each row to format the output.

Nested loops can become complex, especially when dealing with larger data structures or multiple levels of nesting. It's important to keep track of the indentation and the variables used in each loop to avoid confusion and logical errors.

8.2 While loop in python

A while loop in Python is a control flow statement that repeatedly executes a block of code as long as a given condition is true. Unlike a for loop, which iterates over a sequence, a while loop keeps executing its code block until the specified condition becomes false. This is particularly useful when you don't know the exact number of iterations in advance or when you want to create a loop that continues until a specific condition is met.

Here's the structure of a while loop:

```
while condition:
    # Code block to be executed as long as the condition is true
```

Let's break down the key points of a **while** loop:

Initialization: Before entering the loop, you typically initialize variables that will be used to evaluate the loop condition or control the loop's behavior.

Condition: The loop continues executing as long as the condition provided after the **while** keyword is evaluated as **True**.

Code Block: The indented code block under the **while** statement is the body of the loop. It contains the instructions that are executed repeatedly until the condition becomes **False**.

Updating Loop Variables: Inside the loop, you should update the variables involved in the condition to ensure that the condition eventually becomes **False**. Failing to update the variables correctly can lead to an infinite loop.

Termination: The loop terminates when the condition becomes **False**. If the condition is **False** from the start, the loop body might not execute at all.

Now, let's go through an example to illustrate each point:

Example: Printing numbers from 1 to 5 using a **while** loop.

```
num = 1  # Initialization
while num <= 5:  # Condition
   print(num)  # Code block
   num += 1  # Updating loop variable
```

Output:

```
1
2
3
4
5
```

In this example:

Initialization: We set **num** to 1.

Condition: The loop continues as long as **num** is less than or equal to 5.

Code Block: The code block inside the loop prints the value of **num**.

Updating Loop Variable: After each iteration, we increment **num** by 1.

Termination: The loop terminates when **num** becomes 6, causing the condition to become **False**.

Be cautious when using **while** loops, as incorrect initialization or updating of loop variables can lead to infinite loops that don't terminate. Always ensure that the condition will eventually become **False** to avoid such situations.

Here's another example of using a **while** loop:

Example: Calculating the factorial of a number using a **while** loop.

```
number = int(input("Enter a number: "))  # Initialization
factorial = 1  # Initialization
while number > 1:  # Condition
   factorial *= number  # Code block
   number -= 1  # Updating loop variable
print("Factorial:", factorial)
```

Output:

```
Enter a number: 5
Factorial: 120
```

In this example:

Initialization: We take an input from the user and assign it to the **number** variable. We also initialize the **factorial** variable to 1.

Condition: The loop continues as long as **number** is greater than 1.

Code Block: The code block inside the loop updates the **factorial** by multiplying it with the current value of **number**.

Updating Loop Variable: After each iteration, we decrement **number** by 1.

Termination: The loop terminates when **number** becomes 1, causing the condition to become **False**.

This example demonstrates how to use a **while** loop to calculate the factorial of a given number by repeatedly multiplying the current value of the **factorial** variable with the decreasing values of **number**.

8.2.1 Break statement

The **break** statement in a **while** loop in Python is used to immediately exit the loop when a certain condition is met. It's a control flow statement that provides a way to prematurely terminate the loop's execution before the loop condition becomes false. The **break** statement is particularly useful when you want to stop the loop when a specific goal is achieved or a certain condition is satisfied.

Here's how the **break** statement works in a **while** loop:

```
while condition:
   # Loop body
   if some_condition:
      break  # Exit the loop immediately
```

Let's explore the key points of using the **break** statement in a **while** loop:

Loop Initialization: You should initialize variables before entering the loop that will help you evaluate the loop condition and control the loop's behavior.

Loop Condition: The loop continues to execute as long as the condition after the **while** keyword is evaluated as **True**.

Loop Body: The indented code block under the **while** statement is the body of the loop. It contains the instructions that are repeatedly executed until the condition becomes **False**.

Checking a Condition: Inside the loop body, you can use an **if** statement to check for a specific condition. When that condition is met, the **break** statement is executed, and the loop terminates immediately.

Termination: The loop terminates as soon as the **break** statement is executed, regardless of whether the loop condition is still **True**.

Now, let's look at two examples to illustrate the use of the **break** statement in a **while** loop:

Example 1: Searching for a specific number using a **while** loop.

```
numbers = [3, 6, 9, 12, 15]
search_number = 12
index = 0
while index < len(numbers):
    if numbers[index] == search_number:
        print(search_number, "found at index", index)
        break
    index += 1
else:
    print(search_number, "not found in the list.")
```

Output:

12 found at index 3

In this example, the loop iterates through the **numbers** list and checks if the current number matches the **search_number**. If the **search_number** is found, the **break** statement is executed, and the loop terminates immediately.

Example 2: Calculating the sum of numbers until a negative number is encountered.

```
total = 0
while True:
    num = int(input("Enter a number: "))
    if num < 0:
        break
    total += num
print("Total:", total)
```

In this example, the loop keeps asking the user to enter numbers. If the user enters a negative number, the loop terminates immediately using the **break** statement. Otherwise, the input number is added to the **total**.

The **break** statement provides a way to control the flow of your loop and exit early when certain conditions are met. However, be careful not to overuse it, as too many **break** statements can make your code harder to read and debug.

8.2.2 Continue Statement

The **continue** statement in a **while** loop in Python is used to skip the remaining code inside the current iteration of the loop and move on to the next iteration. It's a control flow statement that allows you to effectively "skip" certain steps of the loop's execution based on a specific condition. After encountering the **continue** statement, the loop proceeds to the next iteration, skipping any code that follows the **continue**.

Here's how the **continue** statement works in a **while** loop:

```
while condition:
    # Loop body
    if some_condition:
        continue  # Skip the remaining code and move to the next iteration
```

Now, let's explore the main points of using the **continue** statement in a **while** loop:

Loop Initialization: You should initialize variables before entering the loop that will help you evaluate the loop condition and control the loop's behavior.

Loop Condition: The loop continues to execute as long as the condition after the **while** keyword is evaluated as **True**.

Loop Body: The indented code block under the **while** statement is the body of the loop. It contains the instructions that are repeatedly executed until the condition becomes **False**.

Checking a Condition: Inside the loop body, you can use an **if** statement to check for a specific condition. When that condition is met, the **continue** statement is executed, and the loop immediately proceeds to the next iteration, skipping any remaining code in the current iteration.

Iteration Continuation: After encountering the **continue** statement, the loop doesn't exit; instead, it moves on to the next iteration and evaluates the loop condition again.

Now, let's look at two examples to illustrate the use of the **continue** statement in a **while** loop:

Example 1: Skipping odd numbers in a loop.

```
num = 1
while num <= 10:
    if num % 2 == 1:
        num += 1
        continue
    print("Even number:", num)
    num += 1
```

Output:

```
Even number: 2
Even number: 4
Even number: 6
Even number: 8
Even number: 10
```

In this example, the loop iterates through numbers from 1 to 10. When an odd number is encountered, the **continue** statement is executed, and the loop immediately proceeds to the next iteration, skipping the print statement for odd numbers.

Example 2: Skipping specific values in a loop.

```
values = [5, 7, 8, 3, 12, 6]
for value in values:
    if value == 3 or value == 8:
        continue
    print("Processed value:", value)
```

Output:

```
Processed value: 5
Processed value: 7
Processed value: 12
Processed value: 6
```

In this example, the loop iterates through the **values** list. When a value of 3 or 8 is encountered, the **continue** statement is executed, and the loop immediately proceeds to the next iteration, skipping the print statement for those specific values.

The **continue** statement can be useful when you want to skip specific iterations based on certain conditions, allowing you to focus on the relevant steps of the loop's execution.

8.2.3 Else in While loop

In Python, the **else** statement can be used with a **while** loop to specify a block of code that should be executed after the loop completes normally (without being interrupted by a **break** statement). The **else** block will only execute if the loop condition becomes **False** and the loop completes all iterations. This can be useful when you want to perform an action after the loop has finished its execution, but only if the loop wasn't terminated by a **break** statement.

Here's the structure of using **else** with a **while** loop:

```
while condition:
    # Loop body
else:
    # Code to execute if the loop completes normally (without a break)
```

Let's break down the key aspects of using the **else** statement with a **while** loop:

Loop Initialization: You should initialize variables before entering the loop that will help you evaluate the loop condition and control the loop's behavior.

Loop Condition: The loop continues to execute as long as the condition after the **while** keyword is evaluated as **True**.

Loop Body: The indented code block under the **while** statement is the body of the loop. It contains the instructions that are repeatedly executed until the condition becomes **False**.

Loop Completion: If the loop's condition becomes **False**, indicating that the loop has completed its iterations, the code in the **else** block will be executed.

Break Statement: If the loop is terminated by a **break** statement, the code in the **else** block will not execute.

Here's an example to illustrate the use of the **else** statement with a **while** loop:

Example: Finding the factorial of a number using a **while** loop with an **else** block.

```
number = int(input("Enter a number: "))
factorial = 1
while number > 1:
    factorial *= number
    number -= 1
else:
    print("Factorial:", factorial)
```

In this example:

- Initialization: We take an input from the user and assign it to the **number** variable. We also initialize the **factorial** variable to 1.
- Condition: The loop continues as long as **number** is greater than 1.
- Code Block: The code block inside the loop calculates the factorial of the number by repeatedly multiplying the current value of **factorial** with the decreasing values of **number**.
- Termination: The loop terminates when **number** becomes 1.
- Else Block: After the loop completes normally (when **number** becomes 1), the **else** block is executed, printing the calculated factorial.

It's important to note that the **else** block in a **while** loop will only execute if the loop completes all iterations without encountering a **break** statement. If a **break** statement is encountered, the loop will terminate early, and the **else** block won't execute.

Here's another example using the **else** statement with a **while** loop:

Example: Finding prime numbers in a range using a **while** loop with an **else** block.

```
start = int(input("Enter the start of the range: "))
end = int(input("Enter the end of the range: "))

print("Prime numbers in the range:", start, "to", end)
while start <= end:
    if start <= 1:
        start += 1
        continue

    is_prime = True
    divisor = 2
    while divisor <= int(start ** 0.5):
        if start % divisor == 0:
            is_prime = False
            break
        divisor += 1

    if is_prime:
        print(start, end=" ")

    start += 1
else:
    print("\nPrime number search complete.")
```

In this example:

- Initialization: We take inputs for the start and end of the range from the user.
- Loop Body: The outer loop iterates through numbers in the specified range.
- Skipping 1 and Non-Positive Numbers: We skip numbers less than or equal to 1 using the **continue** statement to avoid incorrect results.
- Prime Number Check: For each number greater than 1, we use a nested **while** loop to check if it's prime by testing for divisors up to the square root of the number.
- Printing Prime Numbers: If a number is found to be prime, it's printed.
- Else Block: After the loop completes normally (when all numbers in the range are checked), the **else** block is executed to indicate the end of the search.

Note that this example is for illustrative purposes. While using nested loops for prime number checking might not be the most efficient approach for large ranges, it demonstrates how to use the **else** statement with a **while** loop to perform an action after completing all iterations.

8.3 Python Functions

In Python, a function is a reusable block of code that performs a specific task or set of tasks. Functions are a fundamental concept in programming as they allow you to organize and modularize your code, making it more readable, maintainable, and efficient. Functions help you avoid writing duplicate code and promote the principle of "Don't Repeat Yourself" (DRY).

Functions in Python have the following characteristics:

Function Definition: You define a function using the def keyword, followed by the function name, a pair of parentheses (), and a colon : to indicate the start of the function's code block.

Function Name: The function name is a user-defined identifier that should follow naming conventions and be descriptive of what the function does.

Parameters: Inside the parentheses of the function definition, you can list parameters (also known as arguments) that the function accepts. Parameters act as placeholders for values that you pass when you call the function.

Function Body: The indented code block following the colon contains the statements that make up the function's logic. This block is executed when the function is called.

Return Value: You can use the return statement to specify the value that the function should produce as its output. If a function doesn't explicitly contain a return statement, it returns None by default.

Function Call: To use a function, you call it by its name followed by parentheses. You can pass arguments to the function inside the parentheses.

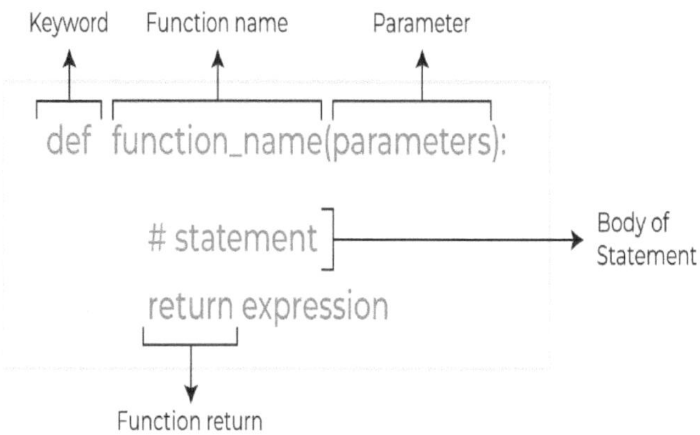

Here's the basic syntax of defining and using a function:

```
def function_name(parameters):
    # Function body
    return result

# Function call
result = function_name(arguments)
```

Now, let's look at a simple example:

```
def greet(name):
    return f"Hello, {name}!"

message = greet("Alice")
print(message) # Output: Hello, Alice!
```

In this example, the **greet** function takes a **name** parameter and returns a greeting message. The function is then called with the argument **"Alice"**, and the returned message is printed.

Functions can also have default parameter values, variable-length argument lists, and keyword arguments, allowing for greater flexibility in how you use and define them. They are an essential building block of Python programming and facilitate the creation of structured and organized code.

8.3.1 Function Parameters:

Parameters are placeholders for values that a function expects to receive when it is called. They allow you to pass information into the function. There are different types of parameters:

- **Positional Parameters**: These are the most common type of parameters. They are defined in the order they appear in the function's parameter list.
- **Default Parameters**: You can assign default values to parameters. If an argument is not provided when calling the function, it will use the default value.
- **Variable-Length Parameters**: If you don't know how many arguments will be passed to the function, you can use ***args** to collect all additional positional arguments into a tuple.
- **Keyword Parameters**: You can specify arguments by name, allowing you to provide arguments out of order.

Here's an example demonstrating these parameter types:

```
def example_function(a, b=10, *args, **kwargs):
    print("a:", a)
    print("b:", b)
    print("args:", args)
    print("kwargs:", kwargs)

example_function(1)
example_function(1, 2, 3, 4, 5, key1='value1', key2='value2')
```

There are different types of function parameters in Python:

Positional Parameters: These are the most common type of parameters. They are defined in the function's signature, and their values are determined by the order in which you provide arguments when calling the function.

```
def greet(name, age):
    print(f"Hello, {name}! You are {age} years old.")

greet("Alice", 30)  # Positional arguments: "Alice" is assigned to 'name', 30 is assigned to 'age'
```

Default Parameters: You can assign default values to parameters in case the caller doesn't provide them. Default parameters must be defined after non-default parameters.

```
def greet(name, age=25):
    print(f"Hello, {name}! You are {age} years old.")

greet("Bob")  # Uses default value for 'age'
greet("Charlie", 28)  # Overrides default value for 'age'
```

Variable-Length Positional Parameters (*args): If you're uncertain how many arguments will be passed to a function, you can use the ***args** parameter to collect all additional positional arguments into a tuple.

```
def print_args(*args):
    for arg in args:
        print(arg)

print_args("apple", "banana", "cherry")
```

Keyword Parameters (kwargs)**: You can use the double-asterisk syntax to collect additional keyword arguments into a dictionary. def print_kwargs(**kwargs):

```
    for key, value in kwargs.items():
        print(key, ":", value)

print_kwargs(name="Alice", age=30, city="New York")
```

Combining Parameter Types: You can use a combination of these parameter types in a function definition.

```
def example(a, b=10, *args, **kwargs):
    print("a:", a)
    print("b:", b)
    print("args:", args)
    print("kwargs:", kwargs)

example(1)  # 'a' takes 1, 'b' takes the default value 10, 'args' and 'kwargs' are empty
example(1, 2, 3, 4, 5, key1='value1', key2='value2')  # 'a' takes 1, 'b' takes 2, 'args' contains (3, 4, 5), 'kwargs' contains
{'key1': 'value1', 'key2': 'value2'}
```

Understanding and using different types of function parameters allows you to create more versatile and adaptable functions that can handle a variety of input data and scenarios.

8.3.2 Function Return Values:

Functions can return values using the return statement. A function can have multiple return statements, but once a return statement is executed, the function exits immediately.

```
def add(a, b):
  return a + b

result = add(3, 5)
print(result) # Output: 8
```

In Python, function return values are the values that a function sends back to the caller after it completes its execution. When you call a function, you can assign its return value to a variable, use it in an expression, or perform any other operation with it.

Here's how you use return values in Python functions:

Return Statement: You use the **return** statement to specify the value that the function should produce as its output. After encountering a **return** statement, the function exits immediately, and the specified value is returned to the caller.

```
def add(a, b):
  return a + b

result = add(3, 5)
print(result) # Output: 8
```

Returning Multiple Values: You can return multiple values from a function using tuples, lists, or other iterable data structures.

```
def calculate(a, b):
  sum_result = a + b
  diff_result = a - b
  return sum_result, diff_result

sum_result, diff_result = calculate(10, 5)
print("Sum:", sum_result) # Output: Sum: 15
print("Difference:", diff_result) # Output: Difference: 5
```

Returning Early: A function can have multiple **return** statements. Once a **return** statement is executed, the function exits immediately, and the value is returned. This is useful when a certain condition is met, and the rest of the function logic is unnecessary.

```
def absolute_value(x):
  if x < 0:
    return -x
  return x

print(absolute_value(-5)) # Output: 5
print(absolute_value(3)) # Output: 3
```

Returning None: If a function doesn't contain a **return** statement or contains a **return** statement without a value, it returns **None** by default. This is often seen in functions that have side effects but don't necessarily compute a result.

```
def greet(name):
  print(f"Hello, {name}!")

result = greet("Alice")
print(result) # Output: None
```

Understanding how to use return values effectively allows you to create functions that perform computations, make decisions, and provide useful information to the caller. Return values make your code more modular and allow you to build complex systems by combining smaller functions.

8.4 Scope and Lifetime of Variables:

Variables defined within a function are considered local variables and are only accessible within that function's scope. Variables defined outside of any function are considered global variables and can be accessed anywhere in the script.

```
global_var = 10

def my_function():
    local_var = 5
    print(global_var)  # Accessing global variable is possible

my_function()
print(local_var)  # This will raise an error since local_var is not in this scope
```
Local Scope: Variables defined within a function are considered local variables. They can only be accessed within the function where they are defined. Once the function exits, the local variables are destroyed, and their memory is released.
```
def my_function():
    local_var = 10  # Local variable
    print(local_var)

my_function()
print(local_var)  # Raises an error because local_var is not accessible here
```
Enclosing Scope: If you have nested functions, the outer function's variables can be accessed within the inner function, but not vice versa.
```
def outer_function():
    outer_var = 5  # Enclosing variable
    def inner_function():
        print(outer_var)
    inner_function()

outer_function()  # Output: 5
```
Global Scope: Variables defined outside any function or block are considered global variables. They can be accessed from anywhere in the code, but if you want to modify them within a function, you need to use the **global** keyword.
```
global_var = 20  # Global variable

def my_function():
    print(global_var)

my_function()  # Output: 20
```
Built-in Scope: Variables that are part of Python's built-in namespace, like **print()**, **len()**, etc., are accessible from any part of your code.
```
print(len([1, 2, 3]))  # Output: 3
```
Lifetime of Variables: The lifetime of a variable depends on its scope. Local variables live as long as the function is executing. Global variables live as long as the program is running. When the variable goes out of scope (i.e., the function ends), its memory is released.

It's important to note that modifying global variables within a function might lead to confusion and make the code harder to understand and maintain. It's generally better to pass variables as arguments to functions and return results, rather than using global variables directly.

Understanding variable scope and lifetime helps you manage your code's structure, avoid naming conflicts, and ensure that variables are used appropriately within their intended contexts.

Docstrings:

Docstrings are string literals that are used to provide documentation for functions, classes, and modules. They can be accessed using the **__doc__** attribute of the respective object.
```
def greet(name):
    """
    This function greets the person passed as an argument.
    """
    return f"Hello, {name}!"
print(greet.__doc__)  # Output: This function greets the person passed as an argument.
```
Anonymous Functions (Lambda Functions):

Lambda functions are small, unnamed functions defined using the **lambda** keyword. They are often used for simple operations and can be passed as arguments to other functions.

```
double = lambda x: x * 2
print(double(5)) # Output: 10
```

Recursion:

Recursion is the process of a function calling itself. It's a powerful technique, especially for solving problems that can be broken down into smaller subproblems.

```
def factorial(n):
  if n == 0 or n == 1:
    return 1
  else:
    return n * factorial(n - 1)

print(factorial(5)) # Output: 120
```

Python functions are versatile tools that allow you to create organized, reusable, and efficient code. By understanding and utilizing function concepts effectively, you can build complex programs while maintaining readability and ease of maintenance.

***args** and ****kwargs**

In Python, ***args** and ****kwargs** are special syntax used in function definitions to accept a variable number of positional and keyword arguments, respectively. They are often used when you want to create flexible and versatile functions that can handle different numbers of arguments without explicitly specifying them in the function signature.

***args (Variable-Length Positional Arguments)**:

The ***args** parameter collects any number of positional arguments passed to the function into a tuple. This allows you to work with the arguments as a sequence.

```
def my_function(*args):
  for arg in args:
    print(arg)
my_function("apple", "banana", "cherry")
# Output:
# apple
# banana
# cherry
```

****kwargs (Variable-Length Keyword Arguments)**:

The ****kwargs** parameter collects any number of keyword arguments passed to the function into a dictionary. This allows you to work with named arguments and their corresponding values.

```
def print_kwargs(**kwargs):
  for key, value in kwargs.items():
    print(key, ":", value)
print_kwargs(name="Alice", age=30, city="New York")
# Output:
# name : Alice
# age : 30
# city : New York
```

Combining ***args** and ****kwargs** in a function allows you to create functions that accept a mix of both positional and keyword arguments, making them highly flexible.

```
def example_function(a, b, *args, **kwargs):
  print("a:", a)
  print("b:", b)
  print("args:", args)
  print("kwargs:", kwargs)
example_function(1, 2, 3, 4, 5, key1='value1', key2='value2')
# Output:
# a: 1
# b: 2
# args: (3, 4, 5)
# kwargs: {'key1': 'value1', 'key2': 'value2'}
```

Using ***args** and ****kwargs** is particularly useful when creating utility functions, decorators, or functions that need to accept a dynamic number of arguments without imposing strict limitations on their usage. However, be mindful of maintaining code readability and documentation, as functions with too many variable arguments can become harder to understand.

8.5 Yield and return in python

In Python, both yield and return are used to send values from a function back to the caller. However, they serve different purposes and are used in different contexts.

Use return when:

1. You want to send a value back to the caller and terminate the function's execution.
2. The function's primary purpose is to perform a computation and provide a result.

```
def calculate_sum(a, b):
  return a + b

result = calculate_sum(3, 5)
print(result) # Output: 8
```

Use yield when:

1. You want to create a generator, which is a type of iterable that generates values one at a time. Generators are useful for efficiently working with large datasets or sequences.
2. You want to create a function that produces a sequence of values without loading all of them into memory at once.
3. You want to implement lazy evaluation, where values are generated on-the-fly as needed.

```
def generate_even_numbers(limit):
  num = 0
  while num < limit:
    yield num
    num += 2

even_gen = generate_even_numbers(10)
for num in even_gen:
  print(num, end=" ") # Output: 0 2 4 6 8
```

When you use **yield**, the function's state is saved, and it can be resumed later from where it left off when requested by the generator. This allows you to iterate over a potentially infinite sequence of values without the need to generate all of them upfront.

In summary:

Use **return** when you want to provide a result and terminate the function's execution.

Use **yield** when you want to create a generator for generating values one at a time, especially when dealing with large datasets or sequences that don't fit in memory all at once.

Generators

Generators are a powerful concept in Python for creating iterators, which are objects used to iterate over a sequence of values. Generators allow you to generate values on-the-fly, one at a time, without loading the entire sequence into memory. This makes them particularly useful for handling large datasets or sequences that may be memory-intensive.

Generators are created using functions with the yield keyword. When a generator function is called, it doesn't execute the function's body immediately. Instead, it returns a generator object that can be used to control the execution of the generator function step by step.

Here's how you define and use generators in Python:

```
def simple_generator():
  yield 1
  yield 2
  yield 3

gen = simple_generator()
print(next(gen)) # Output: 1
print(next(gen)) # Output: 2
print(next(gen)) # Output: 3
# If we call next(gen) again, it will raise StopIteration since the generator has no more values
```

Generators maintain their state across calls to **next()**, allowing them to resume execution from where they left off. This is crucial for generating values efficiently and lazily.

Generators offer several benefits:

- **Memory Efficiency**: Generators generate values one at a time, which is memory-efficient. They are suitable for working with large datasets or sequences.
- **Lazy Evaluation**: Values are generated on-the-fly as needed, so unnecessary computations are avoided. This is especially useful when dealing with infinite sequences or expensive computations.
- **Simplicity**: Generator functions look similar to regular functions but use **yield** instead of **return**. This makes them easy to understand and implement.
- **Iterability**: Generators are iterable, meaning you can use them in loops, list comprehensions, and other constructs that work with iterables.
- **Pipeline Operations**: Generators can be used in pipeline-style operations, where you chain multiple generators or operations together to process data efficiently.

```
def even_numbers(limit):
    num = 0
    while num < limit:
        yield num
        num += 2

def squared_numbers(nums):
    for num in nums:
        yield num * num

evens = even_numbers(10)
squares = squared_numbers(evens)
for num in squares:
    print(num, end=" ")  # Output: 0 4 16 36 64
```

Reduced Memory Overhead: Unlike lists or other data structures that store all values in memory, generators store only the current value and the state needed to generate the next value. This reduces memory usage.

Generators are a fundamental tool for efficient and scalable programming in Python. They allow you to work with sequences of values without the need to load all the data at once, enabling you to process and manipulate large amounts of data effectively.

Summary

Functions: Functions group code for specific tasks, enhancing reusability and structure. They accept input parameters, process data, and can return results. Functions promote maintainability and readability.

Loops: Loops automate repetitive tasks. for loops iterate over sequences, executing code for each element. while loops execute code as long as a condition is true. Loops are vital for efficient data processing.

In essence, functions and loops are essential programming tools that improve code organization, reusability, and efficiency.

- **For Loop:** The **for** loop iterates over a sequence (such as a list, tuple, or range) and executes a block of code for each element in the sequence.
- **While Loop:** The **while** loop repeatedly executes a block of code as long as a specified condition is true.
- **Iteration:** Loops enable efficient iteration over data, performing the same set of operations on each element.
- **Break and Continue:** The **break** statement exits the loop prematurely, while the **continue** statement skips the current iteration and proceeds to the next one.

Exercise 1:

Multiple Choice Questions (MCQs):

Question 1: What is the primary purpose of using functions in Python?

a) Creating graphical user interfaces

b) Storing large amounts of data

c) Promoting code reusability and organization

d) Defining complex data structures

Question 2: Which loop is best suited for iterating through a predefined range of values?

a) for loop
b) while loop
c) switch loop
d) until loop

Question 3: What does the **return** statement do in a function?

a) Terminates the function
b) Prints the result to the console
c) Returns a value to the caller
d) Declares a new variable

Question 4: Which of the following is not a built-in Python function?

a) print()
b) len()
c) iterate()
d) range()

Question 5: In a **while** loop, what must be ensured to prevent an infinite loop?

a) The loop condition should always be **True**
b) The loop should have no exit conditions
c) The loop should only use **break** statements
d) The loop condition should become **False** eventually

Question 6: What is the purpose of the **break** statement in a loop?

a) To end the program
b) To skip the current iteration
c) To exit the loop prematurely
d) To restart the loop from the beginning

Question 7: Which loop is suitable when the number of iterations is not known beforehand?

a) for loop
b) while loop
c) repeat loop
d) do-while loop

Question 8: In Python, what is the difference between **range(5)** and **range(1, 6)**?

a) They are equivalent
b) **range(5)** starts from 1
c) They are both invalid syntax
d) **range(1, 6)** excludes the endpoint 6

Answer

1. c 2. a 3. c 4. c 5. d 6. b 7. d 8. a

Exercise 2:

True/False Questions:

1. Functions in Python can have multiple return statements.
2. A **for** loop can only iterate over numerical ranges.
3. A **while** loop may not execute at all if the initial condition is False.
4. A **break** statement inside a loop terminates the entire program.
5. The **continue** statement skips the current iteration and proceeds to the next one.

Answer

1. True 2. False 3. True 4. False 5. True

Exercise 3:

Review questions:

Question 1: What is a function in Python, and why are functions useful?

Question 2: How do you define a simple function using the def keyword?
Question 3: What is a function signature, and what does it include?
Question 4: Can a function return multiple values? If so, how?
Question 5: What are function arguments, and how do they differ from parameters?
Question 6: How do default parameter values work in Python functions?
Question 7: What is the scope of variables within a function?
Question 8: What are anonymous functions, and how are they created?
Question 9: How do you pass a list or dictionary as an argument to a function?
Question 10: What are recursive functions, and how do you write one?
Question 11: What are the two primary types of loops in Python?
Question 12: How do you write a basic for loop to iterate over a list?
Question 13: What is the purpose of the range() function in loops?
Question 14: How can you exit a loop prematurely?
Question 15: What does the continue statement do within a loop?
Question 16: How do you iterate over the keys and values in a dictionary?
Question 17: Can you nest loops inside each other? If so, give an example where this would be useful.
Question 18: What are list comprehensions, and how do they relate to loops?
Question 19: How do you write an infinite loop, and when might you use one intentionally?
Question 20: How can you loop through multiple lists simultaneously?

Chapter 9

Arrays as a List

In Python, an array is a collection of elements, each identified by an index or a key. However, Python itself doesn't have a built-in data type specifically called an "array." Instead, Python provides a more versatile data structure called a "list" which serves similar purposes to arrays in other programming languages.

Lists in Python:

Lists are ordered collections of elements.

Elements in a list can be of different data types, including numbers, strings, and even other lists.

Lists are mutable, meaning you can modify, add, or remove elements after the list is created.

Elements in a list are accessed using their index, starting from 0 for the first element.

Lists are created using square brackets **[]**.

Here's a simple example of creating and using a list in Python:

```
# Creating a list
fruits = ["apple", "banana", "orange", "grape"]

# Accessing elements by index
print(fruits[0])  # Output: "apple"
print(fruits[2])  # Output: "orange"

# Modifying elements
fruits[1] = "kiwi"
print(fruits)    # Output: ["apple", "kiwi", "orange", "grape"]

# Adding elements
fruits.append("mango")
print(fruits)    # Output: ["apple", "kiwi", "orange", "grape", "mango"]

# Removing elements
del fruits[2]
print(fruits)    # Output: ["apple", "kiwi", "grape", "mango"]
```

While Python lists are a versatile way to manage collections of data, for certain scenarios that require more advanced mathematical operations or performance optimization, you might want to explore libraries like NumPy, which provide more specialized array-like structures and operations.

9.1 Accessing Elements

Accessing elements in Python refers to retrieving specific values from a data structure, such as lists, tuples, strings, or other iterable objects, using their index or key. This allows you to retrieve and manipulate individual values stored within the data structure. Let's focus on lists since they are a commonly used example.

In Python, you access elements in a list using their index positions. The index starts at 0 for the first element, 1 for the second element, and so on. Here's how you access elements in a list:

```
fruits = ["apple", "banana", "orange", "grape"]

# Accessing individual elements by index
first_fruit = fruits[0]
second_fruit = fruits[1]
third_fruit = fruits[2]

print(first_fruit)  # Output: "apple"
print(second_fruit) # Output: "banana"
print(third_fruit)  # Output: "orange"
```

You can also use negative indices to access elements from the end of the list. For example, -1 refers to the last element, -2 refers to the second-to-last element, and so on:

```
last_fruit = fruits[-1]
second_last_fruit = fruits[-2]
print(last_fruit)       # Output: "grape"
print(second_last_fruit) # Output: "orange"
```

Additionally, you can use slicing to access a range of elements within the list:

```
some_fruits = fruits[1:3]    # Retrieves elements at index 1 and 2
print(some_fruits)           # Output: ["banana", "orange"]

first_three_fruits = fruits[:3] # Retrieves elements from the beginning up to index 3
print(first_three_fruits)     # Output: ["apple", "banana", "orange"]

last_two_fruits = fruits[-2:]  # Retrieves elements from the second-to-last to the end
print(last_two_fruits)        # Output: ["orange", "grape"]
```

Accessing elements in Python involves using index positions to retrieve specific values from inerrable objects like lists.

9.1.1 The Length of an Array

In Python, the concept of getting the length of an array is fundamental when you're working with collections of data, such as lists. The length of an array refers to the number of elements it contains. Let's break down each concept related to the length of an array:

Arrays in Python (Lists): In Python, arrays are represented by the built-in data type called "list". A list is a collection of values that can be of various data types, and it's enclosed in square brackets **[ ]**.

```
numbers = [1, 2, 3, 4, 5]
fruits = ["apple", "banana", "orange", "grape"]
```

Length of an Array (List): The length of an array, also known as the "size" or "count", refers to the number of elements it contains. You can get the length of an array using the built-in **len()** function.

```
numbers = [1, 2, 3, 4, 5]
length = len(numbers) # length will be 5
```

Accessing Elements Using Indices: You can access individual elements of an array using their indices. Indices start at 0 for the first element and increase by 1 for each subsequent element.

```
fruits = ["apple", "banana", "orange", "grape"]
first_fruit = fruits[0] # "apple"
second_fruit = fruits[1] # "banana"
```

Negative Indices and Slicing: You can use negative indices to access elements from the end of the array. Slicing allows you to access a range of elements.

```
fruits = ["apple", "banana", "orange", "grape"]
last_fruit = fruits[-1]       # "grape"
some_fruits = fruits[1:3]     # ["banana", "orange"]
```

Getting the Length: The **len()** function returns the number of elements in an array.

```
fruits = ["apple", "banana", "orange", "grape"]
length = len(fruits) # length will be 4
```

Iterating Through an Array: You can use loops, like **for** loops, to iterate through each element in an array.

```
fruits = ["apple", "banana", "orange", "grape"]
for fruit in fruits:
   print(fruit)
```

Common Use Cases: The length of an array is often used for validation, looping, and various data processing tasks. For example, you might iterate through an array to perform operations on its elements.

```
numbers = [1, 2, 3, 4, 5]
for num in numbers:
   print(num * 2)
```

The length of an array in Python refers to the number of elements it contains, and it's obtained using the **len()** function. This length is crucial for accessing, manipulating, and iterating through array elements.

9.2 Looping Array Elements in python

Looping through array elements (or list elements) in Python is a common task for performing operations on each element of an array. You can achieve this using various types of loops, like the for loop or while loop. Let's explore how to loop through array elements using a for loop:

```
fruits = ["apple", "banana", "orange", "grape"]

# Using a for loop to iterate through the array
for fruit in fruits:
    print(fruit)
```

Output:

```
apple
banana
orange
grape
```

In this example, the **for** loop iterates through each element in the **fruits** array, and in each iteration, the variable **fruit** holds the value of the current element. You can then perform any desired operations using the value of **fruit**.
You can also use the **range()** function if you want to access array elements by index:

```
fruits = ["apple", "banana", "orange", "grape"]

for i in range(len(fruits)):
    print(fruits[i])
```

Output:

```
apple
banana
orange
grape
```

However, using the direct loop through elements using **for fruit in fruits** is more Pythonic and often preferred because it's more readable and concise.
If you need both the index and the value of the element, you can use the **enumerate()** function:

```
fruits = ["apple", "banana", "orange", "grape"]

for index, fruit in enumerate(fruits):
    print(f"Index: {index}, Fruit: {fruit}")
```

Output:

```
Index: 0, Fruit: apple
Index: 1, Fruit: banana
Index: 2, Fruit: orange
Index: 3, Fruit: grape
```

By using loops, you can easily iterate through array elements and perform various operations on each element, making your code more efficient and manageable.
Adding elements to an array (list) in Python involves using different methods to append or insert values at specific positions. Here are some common ways to add elements to an array:
Appending Elements: You can add elements to the end of a list using the append() method.

```
fruits = ["apple", "banana", "orange"]
fruits.append("grape")
print(fruits)  # Output: ["apple", "banana", "orange", "grape"]
```

Extending with Another Array: To add multiple elements to the end of a list, you can use the **extend()** method with another list.

```
fruits = ["apple", "banana"]
```

```
additional_fruits = ["orange", "grape"]
fruits.extend(additional_fruits)
print(fruits)#Output:["apple","banana","orange","grape"]
```
Inserting at a Specific Position: You can use the **insert()** method to add an element at a specific index.
```
fruits = ["apple", "banana", "grape"]
fruits.insert(1, "orange") # Insert "orange" at index 1
print(fruits) # Output: ["apple", "orange", "banana", "grape"]
```
Using Concatenation: You can use the + operator to concatenate two lists, effectively adding the elements of the second list to the first list.
```
fruits = ["apple", "banana"]
additional_fruits = ["orange", "grape"]
combined_fruits = fruits + additional_fruits
print(combined_fruits) # Output: ["apple", "banana", "orange", "grape"]
```
Remember that these methods modify the original list. If you need to create a new list with the added elements and keep the original list unchanged, you should assign the result of these operations to a new variable.
```
fruits = ["apple", "banana"]
new_fruits = fruits + ["orange", "grape"]

print(new_fruits) # Output: ["apple", "banana", "orange", "grape"]
print(fruits)     # Output: ["apple", "banana"]
```
Choose the method that best suits your requirements for adding elements to an array in Python.

9.3 Deleting array element in Python

you can delete elements from an array (list) using various methods. Here are some common ways to delete elements from a list:

Using del Statement: The del statement removes an element from a list at a specific index.
```
fruits = ["apple", "banana", "orange", "grape"]
del fruits[1] # Deletes the element at index 1 (banana)
print(fruits) # Output: ["apple", "orange", "grape"]
```
Using remove() Method: The **remove()** method removes the first occurrence of a specified element from the list.
```
fruits = ["apple", "banana", "orange", "grape"]
fruits.remove("banana")
print(fruits) # Output: ["apple", "orange", "grape"]
```
Using pop() Method: The **pop()** method removes an element at a specified index and returns its value. If no index is provided, it removes the last element.
```
fruits = ["apple", "banana", "orange", "grape"]
removed_fruit = fruits.pop(2) # Removes "orange" at index 2
print(removed_fruit) # Output: "orange"
print(fruits)        # Output: ["apple", "banana", "grape"]
```
Using Slicing: You can use slicing to remove a range of elements from the list.
```
fruits = ["apple", "banana", "orange", "grape", "kiwi"]
fruits = fruits[:2] + fruits[3:] # Removes "orange" at index 2
print(fruits) # Output: ["apple", "banana", "grape", "kiwi"]
```
Using List Comprehension: List comprehension can be used to create a new list without the elements you want to remove.
```
fruits = ["apple", "banana", "orange", "grape"]
fruits = [fruit for fruit in fruits if fruit != "banana"]

print(fruits) # Output: ["apple", "orange", "grape"]
```
Remember that these methods modify the original list. If you want to keep the original list intact while creating a new list with the elements removed, consider creating a copy of the list and applying the deletion methods on the copy.

9.4 Array methods

append()	Adds an element at the end of the list
clear()	Removes all the elements from the list
copy()	Returns a copy of the list
count()	Returns the number of elements with the specified value
extend()	Add the elements of a list (or any iterable), to the end of the current list
index()	Returns the index of the first element with the specified value
insert()	Adds an element at the specified position
pop()	Removes the element at the specified position
remove()	Removes the first item with the specified value
reverse()	Reverses the order of the list
sort()	Sorts the list

In Python, arrays are represented using lists, and lists come with a variety of built-in methods that allow you to perform operations on them. These methods are pre-defined functions that can be called on a list to manipulate its elements, add or remove elements, and perform various operations. Here are some common array (list) methods and their explanations:

append() Method: Adds an element to the end of the list.

fruits = ["apple", "banana"] fruits.append("orange") print(fruits) # Output: ["apple", "banana", "orange"]

extend() Method: Extends the list by appending elements from another list.

fruits = ["apple", "banana"] additional_fruits = ["orange", "grape"] fruits.extend(additional_fruits) print(fruits) # Output: ["apple", "banana", "orange", "grape"]

insert() Method: Inserts an element at a specific index in the list.

fruits = ["apple", "banana", "grape"] fruits.insert(1, "orange") # Inserts "orange" at index 1 print(fruits) # Output: ["apple", "orange", "banana", "grape"]

remove() Method: Removes the first occurrence of a specified element from the list.

fruits = ["apple", "banana", "orange", "banana", "grape"] fruits.remove("banana") print(fruits) # Output: ["apple", "orange", "banana", "grape"]

pop() Method: Removes and returns an element at a specific index. If no index is provided, removes the last element.

fruits = ["apple", "banana", "orange", "grape"] removed_fruit = fruits.pop(2) # Removes "orange" at index 2 print(removed_fruit) # Output: "orange" print(fruits) # Output: ["apple", "banana", "grape"]

index() Method: Returns the index of the first occurrence of a specified element.

fruits = ["apple", "banana", "orange", "grape"] index = fruits.index("banana") print(index) # Output: 1

count() Method: Returns the number of occurrences of a specified element in the list.

fruits = ["apple", "banana", "orange", "banana", "grape"] count = fruits.count("banana") print(count) # Output: 2

sort() Method: Sorts the elements of the list in ascending order.

numbers = [5, 2, 9, 1, 5] numbers.sort() print(numbers) # Output: [1, 2, 5, 5, 9]

reverse() Method: Reverses the order of the elements in the list.

fruits = ["apple", "banana", "orange", "grape"] fruits.reverse() print(fruits) # Output: ["grape", "orange", "banana", "apple"]

These are just a few examples of the many methods available for working with arrays (lists) in Python. Each method is designed to make specific tasks easier and more efficient when dealing with lists and their elements.

Top of Form

Summary

Arrays in Python are specialized data structures that store elements of the same data type, making them efficient for numerical computations and data analysis. The widely-used NumPy library provides enhanced array functionality for scientific tasks.

Homogeneous Data: Arrays hold elements of the same type for efficiency.

NumPy Library: NumPy is a popular library for array operations.

Creation: Arrays are made using **numpy.array()**, with options for sequences or nested lists.

Indexing: Accessing elements with zero-based indexing.

Shape and Dimensions: Arrays can be one-dimensional, two-dimensional, or multi-dimensional.

Element-Wise Ops: Perform math operations on entire arrays without loops.

Broadcasting: Arrays can perform operations on different shapes.

Methods and Functions: NumPy offers various methods for arithmetic, statistics, and linear algebra.

Manipulation: Arrays can be reshaped, transposed, concatenated, and split.

Advantages: Efficient for numerical tasks in scientific computing and data analysis.

Challenges: Arrays are static in size and better suited for homogeneous data.

Arrays, particularly from NumPy, empower efficient numerical work and are crucial in scientific computation and data tasks.

Exercise 1:

Multiple Choice Questions (MCQs):

Question 1: What is a defining characteristic of arrays in Python?

a) They can store elements of different data types.
b) They are dynamically resizable.
c) They are primarily used for text data.
d) They hold elements of the same data type.

Question 2: Which library is commonly used for advanced array operations in Python?

a) pandas
b) matplotlib
c) NumPy
d) SciPy

Question 3: What is the primary advantage of using arrays over lists for numerical computations?

a) Arrays allow elements of different types.
b) Arrays have dynamic resizing.
c) Arrays offer better memory efficiency and speed.
d) Arrays can hold strings and integers together.

Question 4: Which function is used to create an array using the NumPy library in Python?

a) create_array()
b) array()
c) numpy_array()
d) np_array()

Question 5: Arrays support which type of indexing?

a) Arbitrary indexing
b) Negative indexing only
c) Zero-based indexing
d) Character-based indexing

Question 6: What is broadcasting in the context of arrays?

a) Broadcasting is a method of extending the size of an array.
b) Broadcasting allows operations between arrays of different shapes.
c) Broadcasting is a way to combine multiple arrays into one.

d) Broadcasting refers to the process of converting arrays to strings.

Question 7: What does the .shape attribute of an array represent?

a) The number of elements in the array.

b) The data type of the elements in the array.

c) The dimensions of the array (rows and columns).

d) The index of the last element in the array.

Question 8: Which method can be used to perform element-wise multiplication of two arrays in NumPy?

a) multiply()

b) mult()

c) dot()

d) prod()

Answer

1. d 2. c 3. c 4. b 5. c 6. b 7. c 8. a

Exercise 2:

True/False Questions:

Question 1: Arrays in Python can hold elements of different data types.

Question 2: The primary advantage of arrays over lists is their dynamic resizing capability.

Question 3: Broadcasting in arrays refers to performing operations between arrays of different shapes.

Question 4: The .shape attribute of an array indicates the number of elements it contains.

Question 5: The np.concatenate() function can be used to combine arrays along columns.

Answer

1. False 2. False 3. True 4. False 5. True

Exercise 3:

Review questions:

Question 1: What is an array, and how is it similar to or different from a list in Python?

Question 2: How do you declare an array using a list?

Question 3: Can an array (represented as a list) hold elements of different data types?

Question 4: What is the time complexity for appending an element to an array implemented as a list?

Question 5: How do you access elements within an array?

Question 6: What are common methods to manipulate arrays in Python?

Question 7: How do you insert an element at a specific index in an array?

Question 8: Can you remove elements from an array? If so, how?

Question 9: How do you find the index of an element in an array?

Question 10: What is slicing, and how can it be used with arrays?

Question 11: How do you concatenate two arrays?

Question 12: What are some built-in functions that can be used to perform operations on arrays?

Question 13: How do you sort an array?

Question 14: Can you reverse an array without using any built-in functions?

Question 15: How do you convert an array to a string?

Question 16: How do you loop through each element of an array?

Question 17: How would you sum all the integers in an array?

Question 18: Can you have an array of arrays (nested arrays)? If so, how do you access elements?

Question 19: How do you clone or copy an array?

Question 20: What are some advantages and disadvantages of using arrays instead of other data structures like linked lists?

Chapter 10

Object-Oriented Programming(OOP)

Object-Oriented Programming (OOP) is a programming paradigm that structures code around the concept of objects, which are instances of classes. Python is a versatile and popular programming language that strongly supports OOP principles, making it an excellent choice for designing complex and maintainable software systems.

At the heart of OOP in Python are classes and objects. A class is a blueprint or template that defines the attributes (data) and methods (functions) that objects of that class will possess. Objects are instances of classes, and they encapsulate both data and behavior. This encapsulation promotes the fundamental OOP principles of abstraction, encapsulation, inheritance, and polymorphism.

Abstraction allows you to focus on the essential aspects of an object while hiding unnecessary details. Encapsulation ensures that an object's internal state is protected from unauthorized access by using access control mechanisms (public, protected, private). This enhances security and reduces the risk of unintended modifications.

Inheritance enables the creation of new classes based on existing ones. This hierarchical structure promotes code reuse, as subclasses inherit attributes and behaviors from their parent classes. Additionally, subclasses can override or extend inherited methods to tailor behavior to specific requirements.

Polymorphism enables objects of different classes to be treated as instances of a common superclass. This simplifies code design and allows interchangeable use of different objects without needing to know their specific implementations.

Python's OOP capabilities include special methods like **__init__** for object initialization, allowing you to define class constructors. These methods streamline object creation and customization.

By following OOP principles, Python developers can build modular, maintainable, and scalable code. OOP's emphasis on organizing code into meaningful structures aligns well with real-world modeling and facilitates collaborative development. Whether building user interfaces, databases, games, or complex business applications, OOP in Python empowers developers to create software that is both elegant and robust.

Object-Oriented Programming (OOP) is built upon several fundamental concepts that guide the design and implementation of software using objects and classes. These concepts help in creating organized, modular, and efficient code. Here are the basic concepts of OOP:

Class: A class is a blueprint or template that defines the structure and behavior of objects. It encapsulates data (attributes) and methods (functions) that operate on that data. Classes serve as a blueprint for creating multiple instances (objects) with similar characteristics.

Object: An object is an instance of a class. It's a concrete representation of the blueprint defined by the class. Objects have state (attributes) and behavior (methods) associated with them.

Encapsulation: Encapsulation is the practice of bundling data and methods that operate on the data into a single unit (object). It restricts direct access to an object's internal state and enforces controlled access through methods. This enhances security and modularity.

Abstraction: Abstraction focuses on exposing only the relevant features of an object while hiding unnecessary details. It simplifies complex reality by modeling classes and objects based on real-world entities and their interactions.

Inheritance: Inheritance allows you to create a new class (subclass or derived class) based on an existing class (superclass or base class). The subclass inherits attributes and methods from the superclass and can extend or override them. This promotes code reuse and modularity.

Polymorphism: Polymorphism enables objects of different classes to be treated as instances of a common superclass. It allows objects to be used interchangeably, facilitating dynamic behavior and code flexibility. Polymorphism is achieved through method overriding and interface implementation.

Constructor (__init__): The constructor is a special method (**__init__**) in a class that initializes object attributes when an object is created. It sets the initial state of the object and prepares it for use.

Method Overriding: Method overriding occurs when a subclass provides a specific implementation for a method that is already defined in its superclass. This allows customization of behavior in the subclass while retaining the same method signature.

Class and Instance Attributes: Class attributes are shared among all instances of a class and are defined within the class body. Instance attributes are unique to each instance and are initialized in the constructor. They encapsulate the object's data.

Access Modifiers: Access modifiers determine the visibility of attributes and methods. Python uses naming conventions like **_variable** (protected) and **__variable** (private) to indicate access levels. However, Python doesn't enforce strict access control.

OOP concepts provide a structured approach to designing software, facilitating code organization, reusability, and maintainability. By using classes and objects to model real-world entities and interactions, OOP enhances code clarity and encourages a modular and collaborative development approach.

10.1 Object and classes

let's explore the concept of classes and objects in Python with proper syntax and examples:

Classes:

A class is a blueprint that defines the structure and behavior of objects. It encapsulates attributes (data) and methods (functions) that the objects created from the class will have.

Syntax of class definition:

```
class ClassName:
    # Class attributes
    class_var = 0

    # Constructor (__init__ method)
    def __init__(self, attribute1, attribute2):
        self.attribute1 = attribute1
        self.attribute2 = attribute2

    # Class methods
    def method1(self):
        # Method logic

    def method2(self):
        # Method logic
```

Objects:

An object is an instance of a class. It represents a concrete realization of the class's blueprint, with its own attributes and behavior.

Syntax of object creation:

```
# Create an object of ClassName
obj1 = ClassName(attribute1_value, attribute2_value)
```

Here's an example using classes and objects:

```
class Student:
    # Class attribute
    student_count = 0

    # Constructor
    def __init__(self, name, age):
        self.name = name
        self.age = age
        Student.student_count += 1

    # Method
    def introduce(self):
        print(f"Hello, my name is {self.name} and I'm {self.age} years old.")

# Create objects of Student class
student1 = Student("Alice", 25)
student2 = Student("Bob", 22)

# Call object methods
student1.introduce()  # Output: Hello, my name is Alice and I'm 25 years old.
student2.introduce()  # Output: Hello, my name is Bob and I'm 22 years old.
```

```
# Access class attribute through class and objects
print(Student.student_count)  # Output: 2
print(student1.student_count)  # Output: 2
print(student2.student_count)  # Output: 2
```

In this example, the **Student** class has a constructor (**__init__**) that initializes attributes **name** and **age**, a method **introduce** that prints a greeting, and a class attribute **student_count** that keeps track of the number of student objects created. Two objects, **student1** and **student2**, are created from the **Student** class, each with its own attribute values and the ability to call the **introduce** method.

10.2 Encapsulation

Encapsulation is one of the fundamental principles of Object-Oriented Programming (OOP) that involves bundling data (attributes) and methods (functions) that operate on that data into a single unit (object). Encapsulation enforces access control, ensuring that an object's internal state is protected from unauthorized access or modification from outside the class. This enhances security, reduces the risk of errors, and promotes modular and organized code.

Syntax of Encapsulation:

In Python, encapsulation is achieved using access modifiers and property methods. Access modifiers control the visibility of attributes and methods within a class, and property methods provide controlled access to these attributes.

```
class ClassName:
    def __init__(self):
        self._protected_var = 0  # Protected attribute
        self.__private_var = 0   # Private attribute

    # Getter method for private attribute
    def get_private_var(self):
        return self.__private_var

    # Setter method for private attribute
    def set_private_var(self, value):
        self.__private_var = value

    # Property method for accessing private attribute
    private_var = property(get_private_var, set_private_var)
```

Example of Encapsulation:

Here's an example demonstrating encapsulation in Python:

```
class BankAccount:
    def __init__(self, account_number, balance):
        self._account_number = account_number  # Protected attribute
        self.__balance = balance               # Private attribute

    # Getter method for private attribute
    def get_balance(self):
        return self.__balance

    # Setter method for private attribute
    def set_balance(self, new_balance):
        if new_balance >= 0:
            self.__balance = new_balance
        else:
            print("Balance cannot be negative.")

    # Property method for accessing private attribute
    balance = property(get_balance, set_balance)

# Create an object of BankAccount
account = BankAccount("12345", 1000)
```

```
# Access protected and private attributes using methods and properties
print(account._account_number)    # Output: 12345
print(account.get_balance())    # Output: 1000

# Modify private attribute using setter method
account.set_balance(1500)
print(account.get_balance())    # Output: 1500

# Attempt to set negative balance (will be rejected)
account.set_balance(-500)    # Output: Balance cannot be negative.
```

In this example, the **BankAccount** class demonstrates encapsulation. The **_account_number** attribute is marked as protected using a single underscore, and the **__balance** attribute is marked as private using double underscores. Access to the private attribute is provided through getter and setter methods, and a property method named **balance** allows controlled access to the private attribute without exposing the direct attribute name. This encapsulation prevents direct access to the private attribute and enforces controlled modification of the balance, enhancing data integrity and security.

10.3 Abstraction

Abstraction is a fundamental concept in Object-Oriented Programming (OOP) that involves focusing on the essential aspects of an object while hiding unnecessary details. It provides a simplified and higher-level representation of an object, making complex systems more manageable and easier to understand. Abstraction is achieved through the use of classes, methods, and interfaces, allowing you to model real-world entities and their interactions without exposing all the implementation details.

Syntax of Abstraction:

In Python, abstraction is achieved by defining classes with methods that provide the required functionality. These methods abstract the underlying implementation details from the user.

```
class AbstractClass:
    def abstract_method(self):
        pass

class ConcreteClass(AbstractClass):
    def abstract_method(self):
        # Provide concrete implementation here
```

Example of Abstraction:

Here's an example demonstrating abstraction in Python:

```
from abc import ABC, abstractmethod

class Shape(ABC):
    @abstractmethod
    def area(self):
        pass

class Circle(Shape):
    def __init__(self, radius):
        self.radius = radius

    def area(self):
        return 3.14 * self.radius ** 2

class Rectangle(Shape):
    def __init__(self, width, height):
        self.width = width
        self.height = height

    def area(self):
        return self.width * self.height
```

```
# Create objects of Circle and Rectangle
circle = Circle(5)
rectangle = Rectangle(4, 6)

# Calculate and print areas using abstraction
print("Circle Area:", circle.area())       # Output: Circle Area: 78.5
print("Rectangle Area:", rectangle.area())  # Output: Rectangle Area: 24
```

In this example, the **Shape** class is an abstract class that defines an abstract method **area()**. An abstract method is a method that is declared in the base class but doesn't provide any implementation. Subclasses, such as **Circle** and **Rectangle**, inherit from the **Shape** class and implement the **area()** method according to their specific shapes.

Abstraction allows you to work with high-level concepts without needing to understand the intricate details of each implementation. It simplifies complex systems by providing clear interfaces and reducing unnecessary complexity. By utilizing abstraction, you can design more modular and maintainable code that is easier to extend and adapt to changing requirements.

10.4 Inheritance

Inheritance is a crucial concept in Object-Oriented Programming (OOP) that allows you to create a new class (subclass or derived class) based on an existing class (superclass or base class). The subclass inherits the attributes and methods of the superclass, which promotes code reuse and the organization of related classes in a hierarchy. Inheritance facilitates the creation of more specialized classes that inherit the behaviors and characteristics of more general classes.

Syntax of Inheritance:

In Python, you can achieve inheritance by creating a new class and specifying the superclass within parentheses after the class name.

```
class BaseClass:
    # Attributes and methods of the base class

class SubClass(BaseClass):
    # Additional attributes and methods of the subclass
```

Example of Inheritance:

Here's an example demonstrating inheritance in Python:

```
class Animal:
    def __init__(self, name):
        self.name = name

    def speak(self):
        pass

class Dog(Animal):
    def speak(self):
        return f"{self.name} says Woof!"

class Cat(Animal):
    def speak(self):
        return f"{self.name} says Meow!"

# Create objects of Dog and Cat
dog = Dog("Buddy")
cat = Cat("Whiskers")

# Call the speak method using inheritance
print(dog.speak())  # Output: Buddy says Woof!
print(cat.speak())  # Output: Whiskers says Meow!
```

In this example, the **Animal** class is the base class that defines the common attributes and an abstract **speak** method. The **Dog** and **Cat** classes are subclasses that inherit from the **Animal** class. They provide specific implementations for the **speak** method, tailoring it to the behavior of dogs and cats.

Inheritance allows you to:

Reuse code by inheriting attributes and methods from a superclass.

Specialize classes by adding new attributes and methods to subclasses.
Override methods in subclasses to provide specific behavior.
Organize related classes into a hierarchy, making the code more modular and organized.

It's important to note that Python supports multiple inheritance, allowing a subclass to inherit from multiple superclasses. However, excessive use of inheritance or deep inheritance hierarchies can lead to code complexity and tight coupling, so careful design and consideration are important when utilizing inheritance.

10.5 Polymorphism

Polymorphism is a core concept in Object-Oriented Programming (OOP) that allows objects of different classes to be treated as instances of a common superclass. It enables you to use different classes through a common interface, providing a way to create more flexible and adaptable code. Polymorphism is achieved through method overriding and interface implementation.

Syntax of Polymorphism:

In Python, polymorphism is achieved when multiple classes implement a common method with the same name but different implementations.

```
class Superclass:
    def common_method(self):
        pass

class Subclass1(Superclass):
    def common_method(self):
        # Implementation for Subclass1

class Subclass2(Superclass):
    def common_method(self):
        # Implementation for Subclass2
```

Example of Polymorphism:

Here's an example demonstrating polymorphism in Python:

```
class Shape:
    def area(self):
        pass

class Circle(Shape):
    def __init__(self, radius):
        self.radius = radius

    def area(self):
        return 3.14 * self.radius ** 2

class Rectangle(Shape):
    def __init__(self, width, height):
        self.width = width
        self.height = height

    def area(self):
        return self.width * self.height

# Create objects of Circle and Rectangle
circle = Circle(5)
rectangle = Rectangle(4, 6)

# Calculate and print areas using polymorphism
shapes = [circle, rectangle]
for shape in shapes:
    print("Area:", shape.area())

# Output:
```

```
# Area: 78.5 (Circle's area)
# Area: 24 (Rectangle's area)
```

In this example, the **Shape** class defines a common method **area()**. The **Circle** and **Rectangle** subclasses inherit from **Shape** and provide their own implementations of the **area()** method. Through polymorphism, both **Circle** and **Rectangle** objects can be treated as instances of the common **Shape** superclass. This allows you to create code that can work with various shapes in a uniform way, regardless of their specific implementations.

Polymorphism is useful for:

- Writing more generic and adaptable code that operates on objects without knowing their specific types.
- Creating code that can work with various implementations of the same interface.
- Simplifying code by treating similar objects consistently, regardless of their specific classes.

__init__

A constructor is a special method in Python that is automatically called when an object of a class is created. It initializes the object's attributes and sets up its initial state. The constructor method is named __init__ and is defined within the class.

```
class ClassName:
    def __init__(self, parameter1, parameter2, ...):
        self.attribute1 = parameter1
        self.attribute2 = parameter2
        # Initialize other attributes

# Creating an object of ClassName
obj = ClassName(value1, value2, ...)
```

Example of Constructor (init):

Here's an example demonstrating the use of the constructor in Python:

```
class Person:
    def __init__(self, name, age):
        self.name = name
        self.age = age

# Creating objects of Person class
person1 = Person("Alice", 30)
person2 = Person("Bob", 25)

# Accessing object attributes
print(person1.name)  # Output: Alice
print(person2.age)  # Output: 25
```

In this example, the **Person** class has a constructor **__init__** that takes two parameters: **name** and **age**. Inside the constructor, the **name** and **age** attributes of the object are initialized with the provided values.

When you create an object of the **Person** class, like **person1** and **person2**, the **__init__** method is automatically called, and the attributes **name** and **age** are set based on the arguments you pass during object creation.

Constructors are useful for setting up the initial state of an object, allowing you to provide initial values for attributes and perform any necessary setup operations. They play a crucial role in object-oriented programming and are essential for creating objects with meaningful data and behavior.

10.6 Method overriding

Method overriding is a concept in Object-Oriented Programming (OOP) where a subclass provides a specific implementation for a method that is already defined in its superclass. This allows the subclass to customize the behavior of the inherited method while retaining the same method signature.

Example of Method Overriding:

Here's an example demonstrating method overriding in Python:

```
class Animal:
    def speak(self):
        return "Animal speaks"

class Dog(Animal):
    def speak(self):
        return "Woof!"
```

```
class Cat(Animal):
    def speak(self):
        return "Meow!"

# Create objects of Dog and Cat
dog = Dog()
cat = Cat()

# Call the overridden method
print(dog.speak())  # Output: Woof!
print(cat.speak())  # Output: Meow!
```

In this example, the **Animal** class has a method named **speak()** that provides a generic message. The **Dog** and **Cat** subclasses inherit from **Animal** and override the **speak()** method with their own specific implementations.

When you call the **speak()** method on objects of **Dog** and **Cat** classes, the overridden methods in the subclasses are executed, providing the customized messages "Woof!" and "Meow!" respectively.

Method overriding is useful for:

- Providing specific behaviors in subclasses while maintaining a consistent interface.
- Allowing subclasses to specialize the functionality inherited from the superclass.
- Implementing polymorphism, where objects of different subclasses can be treated uniformly through a common interface.

10.7 Class attributes and instance attributes

In Python, class attributes and instance attributes are used to store data within classes and objects, respectively. They represent different types of data that can be associated with a class and its instances. Let's explore the differences between class attributes and instance attributes:

Class Attributes:

Class attributes are shared among all instances of a class. They are defined within the class body and are accessible through the class itself or any instance of that class. Class attributes are typically used to store data that is common to all instances of the class.

```
class MyClass:
    class_attribute = "This is a class attribute"

obj1 = MyClass()
obj2 = MyClass()

print(obj1.class_attribute)  # Output: This is a class attribute
print(obj2.class_attribute)  # Output: This is a class attribute

print(MyClass.class_attribute)  # Output: This is a class attribute
```

In the above example, **class_attribute** is a class attribute of the **MyClass** class. Both **obj1** and **obj2** can access this attribute, and it's also accessible through the class name itself.

Instance Attributes:

Instance attributes are specific to individual instances of a class. They are defined within the constructor (**__init__** method) and are unique to each object created from the class. Instance attributes are used to store data that varies between different instances of the class.

```
class Person:
    def __init__(self, name, age):
        self.name = name  # Instance attribute
        self.age = age    # Instance attribute

person1 = Person("Alice", 30)
person2 = Person("Bob", 25)

print(person1.name)  # Output: Alice
print(person2.age)   # Output: 25
```

In the above example, **name** and **age** are instance attributes specific to each instance of the **Person** class. Each object (**person1**, **person2**) has its own values for these attributes.

Class attributes are shared among all instances of a class and are defined within the class body.

Instance attributes are specific to individual instances of a class and are defined within the constructor (**__init__** method).

Understanding the distinction between class and instance attributes is important for managing and organizing data within your classes and objects effectively.

10.8 Access modifiers

Access modifiers in Python are used to control the visibility and accessibility of class attributes and methods. They define the level of access that other parts of the program have to these attributes and methods. Python provides three types of access modifiers:

Public Access Modifier (public):

In Python, all attributes and methods are public by default. They can be accessed from anywhere in the program.

No special syntax is required to denote a public attribute or method.

```
class MyClass:
    def __init__(self):
        self.public_var = 0  # Public attribute

    def public_method(self):
        # Public method logic
```

Protected Access Modifier (protected):

Protected attributes and methods are indicated by a single underscore (_) prefix. They can be accessed within the class and its subclasses (inheritors).

The use of a single underscore is a naming convention and doesn't enforce strict access control.

```
class MyClass:
    def __init__(self):
        self._protected_var = 0  # Protected attribute

    def _protected_method(self):
        # Protected method logic
```

Private Access Modifier (private):

Private attributes and methods are indicated by a double underscore (__) prefix. They can only be accessed within the class where they are defined; they are not inherited by subclasses.

The use of a double underscore causes Python to perform name mangling, changing the attribute name to include the class name as a prefix to make it more difficult to accidentally access from outside the class.

```
class MyClass:
    def __init__(self):
        self.__private_var = 0  # Private attribute

    def __private_method(self):
        # Private method logic
```

It's important to note that access modifiers in Python are not as strict as in some other programming languages. Python uses naming conventions and relies on programmers to follow these conventions for encapsulation and access control. The single underscore (_) and double underscore (__) prefixes signal that an attribute or method should be treated as protected or private, respectively. However, Python does not prevent direct access to these attributes; it is a convention for indicating the intended level of access.

Public attributes and methods have no special syntax and are accessible from anywhere.

Protected attributes and methods use a single underscore (_) prefix and are accessible within the class and its subclasses.

Private attributes and methods use a double underscore (__) prefix, are not inherited, and are accessible only within the defining class (with name mangling).

10.9 Class or Static Variables in Python

All objects share class or static variables. An instance or non-static variables are different for different objects (every object has a copy). For example, let a Computer Science Student be represented by a class CSStudent. The class may have a static variable whose value is “cse” for all objects. And class may also have non-static members like name and roll.

In C++ and Java, we can use static keywords to make a variable a class variable. The variables which don't have a preceding static keyword are instance variables. See this for the Java example and this for the C++ example.
A static variable is a variable that is shared among all instances of a class, rather than being unique to each instance. It is also sometimes referred to as a class variable, because it belongs to the class itself rather than any particular instance of the class.
Static variables are defined inside the class definition, but outside of any method definitions. They are typically initialized with a value, just like an instance variable, but they can be accessed and modified through the class itself, rather than through an instance.
class variables (also known as static variables) are variables that are shared among all instances of a class. They are defined within the class but outside of any instance methods. Class variables hold values that are common to all objects created from the class, and changes to these variables are reflected across all instances. They are particularly useful for storing data that should be consistent for all instances of a class.

Defining Class Variables:

Class variables are defined within the class body and are usually placed at the top, outside of any methods. They are shared among all instances of the class and can be accessed using the class name itself or through instances.

```
class MyClass:
    class_variable = "This is a class variable"

obj1 = MyClass()
obj2 = MyClass()

print(obj1.class_variable)    # Output: This is a class variable
print(obj2.class_variable)    # Output: This is a class variable

print(MyClass.class_variable)  # Output: This is a class variable
```

Modifying Class Variables:

Class variables can be modified using the class name. Changes to a class variable are reflected across all instances of the class.

```
class MyClass:
    class_variable = "This is a class variable"

obj1 = MyClass()
obj2 = MyClass()

MyClass.class_variable = "Updated class variable"

print(obj1.class_variable)    # Output: Updated class variable
print(obj2.class_variable)    # Output: Updated class variable

print(MyClass.class_variable)  # Output: Updated class variable
```

Use Cases for Class Variables:
Class variables are useful for storing data that should be consistent for all instances of a class. Some common use cases include:
Constants: Storing constant values shared among instances.
Counters: Keeping track of the number of instances created.
Configuration settings: Sharing configuration options across all instances.
It's important to note that if you modify a class variable using an instance, it will create an instance variable with the same name within that instance. However, it won't affect the original class variable or other instances. To modify the class variable, it's recommended to use the class name directly.
Understanding class variables is important for designing classes that share data across instances and for maintaining consistent behavior throughout your code.

Class method vs Static method in Python

Both class methods and static methods are used to define methods that are associated with a class rather than an instance of the class. However, they serve different purposes and have different behavior. Let's explore the differences between class methods and static methods:
Class Methods:

A class method is a method that is bound to the class itself, rather than to an instance. It takes the class as its first argument (usually named cls). Class methods are defined using the @classmethod decorator.

```
class MyClass:
    class_variable = "This is a class variable"

    @classmethod
    def class_method(cls, arg1, arg2):
        # cls refers to the class itself
        # ...
```

Class methods can access and modify class-level attributes.

They are often used to create utility methods related to the class, such as factory methods or methods that work with class-level data.

They are called on the class itself, not on instances.

10.10 Static Methods:

A static method is a method that is bound to the class and doesn't have access to the class or instance. It's defined using the **@staticmethod** decorator.

```
class MyClass:
    @staticmethod
    def static_method(arg1, arg2):
        # ...
```

Static methods don't have access to instance or class variables.

They are often used for utility functions that don't require access to instance or class-specific data.

They are called on the class itself, not on instances.

Usage Comparison:

```
class MathOperations:
    @classmethod
    def multiply(cls, a, b):
        return a * b

    @staticmethod
    def square(number):
        return number ** 2

result1 = MathOperations.multiply(3, 4)  # Using class method
result2 = MathOperations.square(5)      # Using static method

print(result1)  # Output: 12
print(result2)  # Output: 25
```

In this example, the **multiply** method is a class method that can access class attributes and perform class-specific operations. The **square** method is a static method that doesn't have access to instance or class attributes; it performs a general operation that doesn't depend on class or instance data.

Class methods are used to work with class-level data and can modify class attributes. They take the class as their first argument (**cls**).

Static methods are used for utility functions that don't require access to instance or class attributes. They don't take any special arguments and don't have access to instance or class data.

Summary

Object-Oriented Programming (OOP) is a programming paradigm that structures code around the concept of objects, which bundle data and methods together to represent real-world entities. In Python, OOP is an integral part of the language, and it offers several fundamental concepts that promote code organization, reusability, and modularity.

Classes and Objects: Classes are blueprints that define the structure and behavior of objects. Objects are instances of classes, representing real-world entities. Classes encapsulate data attributes (properties) and methods (functions) that operate on the data.

Encapsulation: Encapsulation promotes data hiding and information protection by restricting direct access to an object's internal details. This is achieved by using access specifiers (public, protected, private) to control visibility.

Inheritance: Inheritance establishes a parent-child relationship between classes. Child classes (subclasses) inherit attributes and behaviors from parent classes (superclasses). This promotes code reuse and hierarchy in code design.

Polymorphism: Polymorphism allows different objects to be treated as instances of a common superclass. It enables methods to have multiple forms based on the specific object type they are invoked on. This facilitates dynamic behavior and flexibility.

Abstraction: Abstraction focuses on presenting only essential features of an object, while hiding unnecessary details. It simplifies complex systems by emphasizing relevant aspects and minimizing complexity.

Exercise 1:

Multiple Choice Questions (MCQs):

Question 1: What is the main goal of Object-Oriented Programming (OOP)?

a) Improving code execution speed
b) Simplifying code complexity
c) Maximizing data storage
d) Minimizing memory usage

Question 2: Which concept in OOP promotes the idea of bundling data and methods that operate on the data into a single unit?

a) Functions
b) Libraries
c) Classes
d) Modules

Question 3: In OOP, what is an instance of a class called?

a) Method
b) Object
c) Argument
d) Variable

Question 4: What is the process of creating a new instance of a class called?

a) Instantiation
b) Inheritance
c) Encapsulation
d) Abstraction

Question 5: Which principle of OOP allows a class to inherit attributes and behaviors from another class?

a) Encapsulation
b) Abstraction
c) Inheritance
d) Polymorphism

Question 6: In Python, which keyword is used to create a new class?

a) type
b) class
c) def
d) new

Question 7: What is the access specifier that allows class members to be accessed from outside the class and its subclasses?

a) private
b) protected
c) public
d) internal

Question 8: What is method overloading in OOP?

a) Creating multiple methods with the same name but different parameters
b) Using methods to overload the system memory
c) Disabling certain methods to avoid overloading
d) Overriding superclass methods with subclass methods

Answer

1. b 2. c 3. b 4. a 5. c 6. b 7. c 8. a

Exercise 2:

True/False Questions:

Question 1: Encapsulation is the practice of hiding implementation details and exposing only necessary functionalities.

Question 2: Polymorphism allows objects of different classes to be treated as objects of the same class through inheritance.

Question 3: Inheritance enables a class to inherit properties and methods from multiple parent classes simultaneously.

Question 4: An object's attributes in OOP can only be accessed using methods.

Question 5: OOP's main goal is to organize code by dividing it into smaller, reusable components.

Answer

1. True 2. True 3. False 4. False 5. True

Exercise 3:

Review questions:

Question 1: What is Object-Oriented Programming (OOP) and how does it differ from procedural programming?
Question 2: What is a class, and how is it different from an object?
Question 3: How do you define a class in Python?
Question 4: What are instance variables and how do they differ from class variables?
Question 5: What is a constructor, and how is it defined in Python?
Question 6: What is encapsulation, and how is it achieved in Python?
Question 7: Can you explain what inheritance is and provide a use case for it?
Question 8: What is polymorphism, and how can it be implemented in Python?
Question 9: What are access modifiers, and what types exist in Python?
Question 10: What is the purpose of the **self** keyword in Python classes?
Question 11: What are class methods and how do they differ from instance methods?
Question 12: What is method overloading and method overriding?
Question 13: How do you create a static method in a Python class, and when would you use one?
Question 14: What are abstract classes, and how do you create one in Python?
Question 15: What is composition in OOP, and how is it different from inheritance?
Question 16: What is the **super()** function used for?
Question 17: What are properties in Python OOP, and how are they useful?
Question 18: Can a class inherit from multiple classes? If so, what is this called?
Question 19: What is the diamond problem in multiple inheritance, and how does Python resolve it?
Question 20: What is the significance of the **__str__** and **__repr__** methods in Python classes?

Chapter 11

Recursion

What is recursion in Python?

Recursion is a programming concept where a function calls itself directly or indirectly in order to solve a problem. In other words, recursion involves breaking down a complex problem into simpler, smaller instances of the same problem until a base case is reached, at which point the recursion starts to "unwind" and the solutions to the smaller instances are combined to solve the original problem.

In Python, recursion is often likened to a Russian nesting doll: each function call opens a smaller, identical doll until you reach the smallest one. At this point, the process reverses, and each doll is closed, or in programming terms, each function call is resolved.

For instance, let's talk about the Fibonacci sequence, a series of numbers in which each number is the sum of the two preceding ones, usually starting with 0 and 1. It's another classic example where recursion shines.

Here's a high-level explanation of how recursion works:

- **Base Case**: Every recursive function must have a base case, which is a condition that specifies when the recursion should stop. It's the simplest form of the problem that can be solved directly without further recursion.
- **Divide and Conquer**: Recursion works by dividing a problem into smaller sub-problems that are similar to the original problem but simpler. Each of these sub-problems is solved by making a recursive call to the same function.
- **Combining Solutions**: As the recursion unwinds (when the base case is reached), the solutions to the smaller sub-problems are combined to form the solution to the original problem.

Recursion is a powerful programming technique, but like any tool, it has its advantages and disadvantages, particularly when used in the context of Python. Let's explore both sides:

Advantages of Recursion in Python:

- **Solving Complex Problems**: Recursion can simplify the solution to complex problems by breaking them down into smaller, more manageable sub-problems. This can lead to cleaner and more understandable code.
- **Elegant Code**: Recursive solutions can often be more elegant and concise compared to iterative solutions, especially for problems that have a recursive nature.
- **Divide and Conquer**: Recursion is particularly useful for problems that can be divided into smaller instances of the same problem. This is a common strategy for solving tasks like tree traversal, searching, and sorting.
- **Mathematical Formulas**: Many mathematical formulas and sequences have recursive definitions, making recursion a natural choice for implementing them.

Disadvantages of Recursion in Python:

- **Memory Usage:** Recursion can consume a significant amount of memory due to the need to store intermediate function calls on the call stack. This can lead to stack overflow errors when dealing with deep or unbounded recursion.
- **Performance:** Recursive calls can be slower than their iterative counterparts due to the overhead of function calls and the potential for repeated calculations.
- **Difficulty in Debugging:** Debugging recursive functions can be challenging, especially when dealing with complex call stacks and multiple instances of the function running simultaneously.
- **Complexity and Readability:** While recursion can lead to elegant solutions, it can also make code harder to understand for those who are not familiar with the concept. Iterative solutions might be clearer in some cases.
- **Lack of Tail Call Optimization:** Python does not optimize tail recursion (a special type of recursion where the recursive call is the last action in the function), which means deep tail-recursive functions can lead to stack overflow errors.
- **Limited Depth:** Python's default recursion depth limit can restrict the maximum depth of recursion. While you can modify this limit, it's not recommended to do so without understanding the potential consequences.

Guidelines for Using Recursion in Python:

- **Base Case:** Always define a clear and reachable base case to stop the recursion. This prevents infinite recursion.
- **Termination Condition:** Ensure that the recursion reaches the base case in a finite number of steps to avoid performance and memory issues.

Tail Recursion: Whenever possible, structure your recursive function to be tail recursive, where the recursive call is the last operation before returning. This can potentially help with optimization.

Testing: Test your recursive function thoroughly with various input cases to ensure it works as expected and doesn't lead to unexpected behavior.

Alternative Approaches: For problems that can be solved both recursively and iteratively, consider both approaches and choose the one that better suits the problem's characteristics and readability.

In conclusion, recursion is a valuable technique in Python and programming in general, but it should be used thoughtfully. It's important to consider the trade-offs and potential drawbacks when deciding whether to use recursion for a particular problem.

11.1 How recursion works?

Recursion is a programming technique in which a function calls itself to solve a problem. It's like a process of solving a big problem by breaking it down into smaller, simpler instances of the same problem. To understand how recursion works, let's go through a step-by-step explanation using a simple example: calculating the factorial of a number.

Factorial of a non-negative integer n (denoted as n!) is the product of all positive integers from 1 to n. For example, 5! = 5 * 4 * 3 * 2 * 1 = 120.

Here's how recursion works for calculating the factorial of a number:

1. Base Case: Every recursive function needs a base case that defines when the recursion should stop. For factorial, the base case is when n is 0 or 1, where n! = 1.
2. Recursive Step: The function will perform some computation using the current input and then make a recursive call to itself with a modified input, moving closer to the base case.

Let's write a recursive function in Python to calculate the factorial of a number:

```
def factorial(n):
    if n == 0 or n == 1:  # Base case
        return 1
    else:
        return n * factorial(n - 1)  # Recursive step

result = factorial(5)
print(result)  # Output: 120
```

Step by step, the recursive calls for factorial(5) are as follows:

factorial(5) calls factorial(4)
factorial(4) calls factorial(3)
factorial(3) calls factorial(2)
factorial(2) calls factorial(1)
factorial(1) returns 1 (base case)

The chain of recursive calls unwinds, and calculations are combined:

factorial(2) receives the value of 1 from the previous call and returns 2 * 1
factorial(3) receives the value of 2 from the previous call and returns 3 * 2
factorial(4) receives the value of 6 from the previous call and returns 4 * 6
factorial(5) receives the value of 24 from the previous call and returns 5 * 24, which is 120

Another explanation of recursion using a code example. Here's a simple example in Python to illustrate how recursion works:

```
def countdown(n):
    if n <= 0:
        print("Blastoff!")
    else:
        print(n)
        countdown(n - 1)

countdown(5)
```

In this example, the function **countdown()** demonstrates recursion by counting down from a given number (**n**) until it reaches or goes below 0. Let's break down how the recursion works step by step:

The initial call is made to **countdown(5)** outside the function.

Inside the function, it checks if **n** is less than or equal to 0. If **n** is less than or equal to 0, it prints "Blastoff!" and the recursion stops.

If **n** is greater than 0, it prints the value of **n** and then makes a recursive call to **countdown(n - 1)**.

The recursive call starts with **n** being 4, and the process repeats until **n** becomes 0.

The sequence of calls and prints looks like this:

```
5
4
3
2
1
Blastoff!
```

As you can see, each call to countdown() invokes the function again with a smaller value of n. The function keeps calling itself until the base case (when n <= 0) is reached, at which point the recursion starts to unwind.

Recursion can indeed simplify certain problems, but as you mentioned, it can also have its drawbacks, such as increased memory usage and difficulty in debugging. It's important to carefully design recursive functions to ensure they have proper base cases and termination conditions to avoid infinite recursion.

11.2 Python recursive function

A recursive function in Python is a function that calls itself to solve a problem. Instead of using iterative constructs like loops, a recursive function breaks down a problem into smaller instances of the same problem and solves each instance by making recursive calls. Recursive functions are based on the concept of mathematical induction, where a problem is solved by solving a smaller version of the same problem.

A recursive function typically consists of two parts:

Base Case: The base case is the simplest form of the problem that can be solved directly without further recursion. It serves as the stopping condition for the recursion.

Recursive Step: In the recursive step, the function performs some computation using the current input and then makes a recursive call to itself with a modified input, moving closer to the base case.

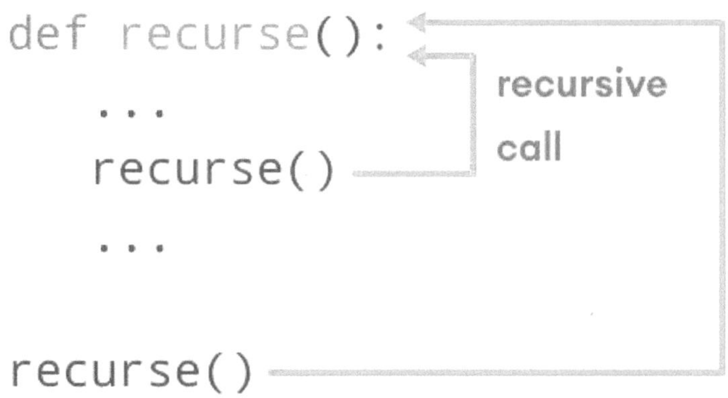

Example of a recursive function

```
def factorial(x):
    """This is a recursive function
    to find the factorial of an integer"""

    if x == 1:
        return 1
    else:
```

```
        return (x * factorial(x-1))


num = 3
print("The factorial of", num, "is", factorial(num))
```

Output

The factorial of 3 is 6

In the above example, factorial() is a recursive function as it calls itself.

When we call this function with a positive integer, it will recursively call itself by decreasing the number.

Each function multiplies the number with the factorial of the number below it until it is equal to one. This recursive call can be explained in the following steps.

```
factorial(3)        # 1st call with 3
3 * factorial(2)    # 2nd call with 2
3 * 2 * factorial(1) # 3rd call with 1
3 * 2 * 1           # return from 3rd call as number=1
3 * 2               # return from 2nd call
6                   # return from 1st call
```

Let's look at an image that shows a step-by-step process of what is going on:

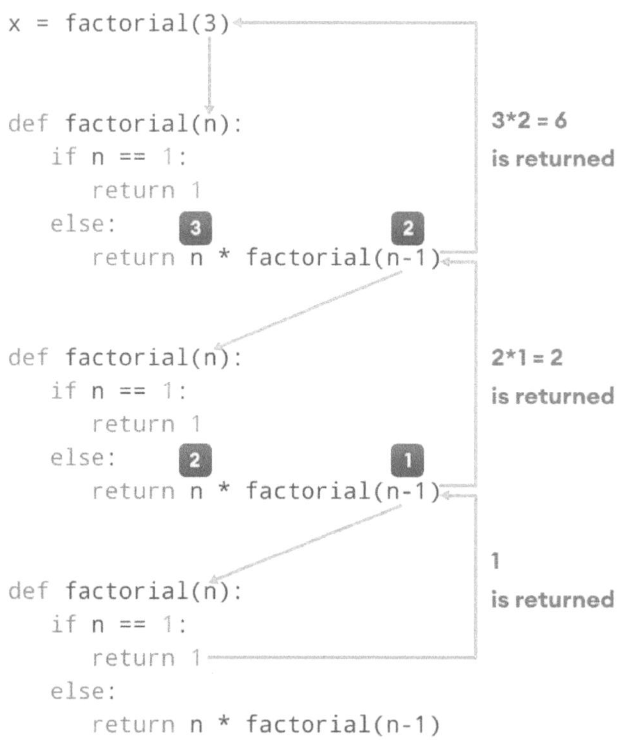

Imagine you're telling a story, and each time you tell a part of the story, you also tell a smaller version of the same story. You keep doing this until the story becomes really tiny and simple, and you know exactly how to finish it without telling any more smaller versions.

Recursion in programming is like telling that story. You have a problem you want to solve, and you break it down into smaller parts of the same problem. You keep doing this until the problem becomes so small that you know the answer right away. This small problem with the answer is like your "base condition" or "base case."

But you need to be careful! Just like in the story, if you keep telling smaller versions forever, you'll never finish. In programming, if you don't have a base case that stops the process, the computer will keep doing the same thing over and over again until it can't handle it anymore. It's like someone talking and talking in the story but never getting to the end.

```
def recursor():
   recursor()

recursor()
```

It's like someone telling the story but forgetting to say how it ends. The function keeps calling itself and making the story smaller, but there's no clear point where it says "stop" or "end." This is a bit like someone in the story talking and talking about the same thing and never moving on to a different part of the story. Eventually, the computer gets tired and says, "I can't do this anymore!" That's when you see the "RecursionError: maximum recursion depth exceeded" message. It's like the computer saying, "I've talked too much and can't remember where I started!"

When using recursion in programming, you need to make sure you have a clear ending point (the base condition) to avoid the computer getting stuck and running out of memory.

11.3 Recession vs iteration

Recursion and iteration are two different approaches used in programming to solve problems. Let's explore the detailed differences between recursion and iteration:

Recursion:

Definition: Recursion involves solving a problem by breaking it down into smaller instances of the same problem.

Function Calls: A recursive function calls itself directly or indirectly to solve the problem. It uses the "divide and conquer" strategy.

Base Case: Every recursive function must have a base case, which is a condition that specifies when the recursion should stop. The base case is the simplest form of the problem that can be solved directly.

Implementation: Recursive solutions are often more elegant and concise, especially for problems with a recursive structure.

Complexity: Recursion can simplify complex problems and make the code more understandable by expressing the problem's nature.

Memory Usage: Recursive calls require memory for each function call, which can lead to increased memory consumption, especially for deep recursion.

Debugging: Debugging recursive functions can be challenging due to the complex call stack. Mistakes can lead to infinite recursion and stack overflow errors.

Iteration:

Definition: Iteration involves solving a problem using loops and repeatedly applying a set of instructions.

Loop Constructs: Iterative solutions use loop constructs such as "for" loops, "while" loops, or "do-while" loops.

Control Flow: Iteration typically involves maintaining control variables to keep track of the loop's progress and terminate it when necessary.

Termination Condition: The termination condition for a loop is explicitly defined within the loop construct.

Implementation: Iterative solutions are often more straightforward for problems that can be broken down into a series of steps.

Complexity: Iteration can be clearer for problems that are not inherently recursive in nature.

Memory Usage: Iteration generally uses less memory compared to recursion because it doesn't involve a growing call stack.

Debugging: Debugging iterative solutions is usually simpler, as the control flow is more direct and there's no risk of infinite recursion.

Choosing Between Recursion and Iteration:

Nature of the Problem: Choose recursion for problems that can be broken down into smaller instances of the same problem. Choose iteration for tasks that require repetitive actions without a clear recursive structure.

Readability: Recursion can lead to more elegant and expressive code for problems with a recursive structure. Iteration might be clearer for tasks that involve straightforward repetition.

Memory Usage: If memory efficiency is a concern, iteration might be preferable, as recursion can lead to a growing call stack and higher memory consumption.

Debugging and Complexity: Iteration is generally easier to debug and can be a better choice for problems where the recursive solution is hard to grasp.

both recursion and iteration have their strengths and weaknesses. The choice between them depends on the problem's characteristics, readability, memory usage, and your familiarity with each approach.

Comparison Basis	**Recursion**	**Iteration**
Implementation	Implemented by a function calling itself	Implemented using loops
State	Defined by parameters values stored in the stack	Defined by control variable value
Syntax	Only termination condition is required	Includes initialization, condition, and increment/decrement of the control variable
Termination	Condition defined within the function body and when this condition becomes true, the recursion ends	Defined within the definition of the loop and when this condition becomes false, the loop terminates
No Termination Statement	In the case of an absence of a base condition, a situation of infinite recursion occurs. In situation can cause stack overflow error or can crash the system	If no termination condition is specified then the infinite loop uses CPU cycles
Code size	Smaller than iteration	Bigger
Speed	Slower due to the overhead of maintaining a stack	Faster
Time complexity	High time complexity	Its time complexity is easier to calculate by calculating the number of times the loop body gets executed. Generally, it has lower time complexity
Comparison Basis	Recursion	Iteration
Implementation	Implemented by a function calling itself	Implemented using loops

11.4 Binary search in Python

Binary search is a search algorithm used to find the position of a target value within a sorted collection, such as an array or a list. It's a very efficient way to search for a specific element, as it significantly reduces the number of comparisons needed compared to linear search.

Here's how binary search works:

1. **Sorted Collection:** Binary search requires the collection to be sorted in ascending or descending order. This sorting is crucial for the algorithm to work correctly.
2. **Divide and Conquer:** The algorithm starts by looking at the middle element of the collection. If the middle element is equal to the target value, the search is successful, and the position of the element is returned.
3. **Comparison:** If the middle element is not equal to the target, the algorithm compares the target value with the middle element. If the target is smaller, it means the target must be in the left half of the collection (because it's sorted), so the search continues in the left half. If the target is larger, the search continues in the right half.
4. **Reducing the Search Interval:** At each step, the algorithm halves the search interval. It repeats this process by selecting the middle element of the remaining interval and comparing it with the target value.
5. **Base Case:** The search continues until the search interval becomes empty, which means the target value is not present in the collection. If the target is found, the algorithm returns the position of the target.

Here's a step-by-step example of binary search for finding the value 11 in a sorted array:

```
sorted_array = [1, 3, 5, 7, 9, 11, 13, 15, 17]
target = 11

left = 0
right = len(sorted_array) - 1

while left <= right:
    mid = (left + right) // 2
    if sorted_array[mid] == target:
        print(f"Target {target} found at index {mid}")
        break
    elif sorted_array[mid] < target:
        left = mid + 1
    else:
        right = mid - 1
else:
    print(f"Target {target} not found in the array")
```

In this example, the algorithm initially selects the middle element (**9**) and compares it to the target value (**11**). Since **11** is larger than **9**, the algorithm narrows the search interval to the right half. The process continues until the target value is found at index **5**.

Binary search is very efficient and has a time complexity of O(log n), where **n** is the number of elements in the collection. This makes it particularly useful for searching large sorted datasets. However, if the collection is not sorted, binary search will not work correctly.

Recursion in Binary search

Recursion can be used to implement binary search as well. Instead of using a loop to repeatedly narrow down the search interval, a recursive function can be used to perform the binary search step by step. Here's how you can implement binary search using recursion:

```
def binary_search_recursive(arr, target, left, right):
    if left <= right:
        mid = (left + right) // 2

        if arr[mid] == target:
            return mid  # Target found at index 'mid'
        elif arr[mid] < target:
            return binary_search_recursive(arr, target, mid + 1, right)
        else:
            return binary_search_recursive(arr, target, left, mid - 1)
    else:
        return -1  # Target not found in the array

# Example usage
sorted_array = [1, 3, 5, 7, 9, 11, 13, 15, 17]
target = 11

result = binary_search_recursive(sorted_array, target, 0, len(sorted_array) - 1)
if result != -1:
    print(f"Target {target} found at index {result}")
else:
    print(f"Target {target} not found in the array")
```

In this recursive implementation:

- The function **binary_search_recursive** takes the array, target value, left index, and right index as parameters.

- The base case checks if **left** is less than or equal to **right**. If not, the search interval has become empty, and the target value is not in the array.
- If the base case is not met, the middle index **mid** is calculated, and the target value is compared with the middle element.
- If the target is found, the middle index is returned. If the target is smaller, the search is continued in the right half of the interval. If the target is larger, the search is continued in the left half.
- The recursive calls narrow down the search interval in each step until the target value is found or the interval becomes empty.

Recursion allows you to express the binary search algorithm in a concise and elegant way, similar to how the algorithm is defined mathematically. However, be mindful of potential stack overflow errors if the recursion depth becomes too large.

11.5 Base Case and Recursive Case

n computer science and programming, recursion is a technique where a function calls itself directly or indirectly to solve a problem. When writing recursive functions, it's crucial to understand two core concepts: the Base Case and the Recursive Case.

Base Case

The Base Case is a condition within the recursive function that tells it when to stop calling itself, thereby preventing an infinite loop. When the base case is met, the function should return a value without making any further recursive calls.

Importance of Base Case:

- Halting Condition: Without a base case, the recursion will continue indefinitely, leading to a stack overflow error.
- Contribution to Final Solution: Usually, the base case's return value is used in calculations for the higher-level recursive calls.

  Example:

For computing the factorial of a number n (denoted as n!), the base case is when n equals 0 or 1. In those cases, n! is 1.

```
def factorial(n):
    if n == 0 or n == 1:  # Base Case
        return 1
    # ... Recursive Case code here ...
```

Recursive Case

The Recursive Case is where the function does its main work and calls itself to solve a smaller instance of the problem. Usually, the recursive case modifies the arguments in some way to ensure that the base case will eventually be reached.

Importance of Recursive Case:

Problem Decomposition: It breaks down the problem into smaller, more manageable pieces.

Combining Solutions: The solutions to the smaller problems are usually combined to form the solution to the original problem.

Example:

Continuing with the factorial example, the recursive case would multiply n by the factorial of n-1.

```
def factorial(n):
    if n == 0 or n == 1:  # Base Case
        return 1
    else:  # Recursive Case
        return n * factorial(n - 1)
```

Putting it all Together:

Here is the complete factorial function using both the base and recursive cases.

```
def factorial(n):
    if n == 0 or n == 1:  # Base Case
        return 1
    else:  # Recursive Case
        return n * factorial(n - 1)
```

Considerations:
Order: Typically, the base case is checked before the recursive case in the function body.
Multiple Base Cases: Some problems may have more than one base case.
Depth of Recursion: Be cautious of the depth to which recursion goes; Python has a maximum recursion depth, often set to 3000.
Efficiency: Sometimes recursion can be inefficient for problems that recompute the same subproblems. In such cases, memorization can be used to store already computed results.
Understanding the base case and the recursive case is fundamental to writing correct and efficient recursive functions in Python or any other programming language.

11.6 Stack Overflow in Python

A stack overflow is an error that occurs when a program's call stack exceeds its size limit. In Python, this often happens during excessively deep or infinite recursion, but it can also occur in deeply nested function calls even if they are not recursive.
How Stack Overflow Occurs:
When a function is called in Python, a stack frame is allocated to handle the function's local variables and to remember the point in the program at which the function was called, so execution can return there once the function is complete. When a function calls itself recursively, a new stack frame is created for each call, piling on top of the previous one. If the recursion is too deep, this stack of frames can grow to the point that it exceeds the stack size limit, causing a stack overflow.
Symptoms:
The most apparent sign of a stack overflow in Python is a RecursionError exception with the message "maximum recursion depth exceeded."
Example:
A classic example of stack overflow in Python is an improperly implemented recursive function without a base case.

```
def infinite_recursion(n):
    return infinite_recursion(n+1)  # Missing base case

infinite_recursion(0)  # Causes RecursionError
```

Running this code will result in the following error message:
RecursionError: maximum recursion depth exceeded
How to Prevent Stack Overflow
Define a Base Case: Make sure every recursive function has a base case that is correctly defined and reachable.
Check Your Logic: Make sure that the function's logic ensures that it will reach its base case(s).
Limit Recursion Depth: You can limit the recursion depth manually using a counter variable or by setting a threshold.
Tail Recursion: Some programming languages optimize tail recursion to prevent stack overflow. However, Python does not optimize for tail recursion.
Iterative Solutions: Consider using iterative solutions for problems that could involve very deep recursion stacks.
Increasing Stack Size: It's generally not recommended, but you can technically change the maximum recursion depth using sys.setrecursionlimit(limit). Note that doing so can be risky.
Mitigation using Memoization:
For recursive algorithms that repeatedly solve the same sub-problems, memoization can be used to store results of these sub-problems to reduce the number of recursive calls, thus lessening the chance of a stack overflow.
Example with Memoization:

```
def factorial(n, memo={}):
    if n in memo:
        return memo[n]
    if n == 0 or n == 1:
        return 1
    memo[n] = n * factorial(n-1, memo)
    return memo[n]
```

Understanding stack overflow is crucial for debugging, as well as for designing algorithms that are both correct and efficient. It's essential to be aware of the risks of deep or infinite recursion, particularly in a language like Python that does not have built-in tail recursion optimization and has a relatively low default limit for maximum recursion depth.

Summary

Recursion is a powerful programming technique in which a function calls itself to solve a problem. It's a fundamental concept used to solve complex problems by breaking them down into simpler, self-referential instances. In Python, recursion offers an elegant way to solve problems that can be divided into smaller subproblems of the same nature.

- Base Case: Recursion involves breaking down a problem into smaller instances, with each instance approaching a base case that doesn't require further recursion. The base case provides a stopping condition.
- Recursive Case: In the recursive case, a function calls itself with a modified input or state. Each recursive call brings the problem closer to the base case.
- Memory Usage: Recursive functions use the call stack to keep track of function calls and return values. Excessive recursion without a base case can lead to a stack overflow.
- Factorial Example: Calculating the factorial of a number using recursion is a classic example. The base case is when the number is 0 or 1, and the recursive case involves multiplying the number with the factorial of (number - 1).
- Fibonacci Sequence: The Fibonacci sequence is another common example. It demonstrates how a problem can be divided into two subproblems, each involving a recursive call.
- Indirect Recursion: Indirect recursion occurs when multiple functions call each other in a circular manner to achieve a certain computation.
- Advantages: Recursion can provide elegant solutions to complex problems by breaking them down into smaller, more manageable parts.
- Disadvantages: Recursive solutions can be memory-intensive due to the call stack and may be less efficient for some problems compared to iterative solutions.

Exercise 1:

Multiple Choice Questions (MCQs):

Question 1: What is recursion in programming?
a) A loop that repeats a specific code block
b) A technique of defining a function within another function
c) A method of solving complex problems by dividing them into simpler instances
d) A way to define classes and objects in object-oriented programming

Question 2: What is a base case in a recursive function?
a) The point where the program terminates
b) A case that involves the most complex problem
c) The case where the function calls itself
d) A case where the function returns a value

Question 3: Which of the following examples can be effectively solved using recursion?
a) Simple arithmetic calculations
b) Sorting an array of integers
c) Finding the sum of digits in a number
d) Printing a list of elements

Question 4: What happens if a recursive function lacks a proper base case?
a) The function returns an incorrect value.
b) The function produces a syntax error.
c) The function enters an infinite loop.
d) The function doesn't execute any code.

Question 5: In a recursive function, what is the role of the recursive call?
a) It initializes the function's variables.
b) It prevents the base case from being reached.
c) It helps in performing iterative operations.
d) It solves a smaller subproblem of the same nature.

Question 6: Which example represents an indirect recursion scenario?
a) A function calling itself with different arguments
b) Two functions calling each other in a circular manner

c) A function calling multiple other functions
d) A function modifying its arguments before calling itself

Question 7: Which data structure is commonly used to implement recursion?
a) Stack
b) Queue
c) Linked list
d) Array

Question 8: What is the primary advantage of using recursion in solving problems?
a) It guarantees faster execution compared to loops.
b) It simplifies complex problems without dividing them.
c) It reduces memory usage compared to iterative solutions.
d) It provides an elegant and intuitive solution for certain problems.

Answer

1. c 2. a 3. c 4. c 5. d 6. b 7. a 8. b

Exercise 2:

True/False Questions:

Question 1: Recursion involves a function calling itself.
Question 2: Every recursive function requires a base case to terminate the recursion.
Question 3: Recursion is an efficient solution for all types of programming problems.
Question 4: A recursive function is always faster and uses less memory than an iterative equivalent.
Question 5: In recursion, the stack keeps track of function calls and their respective local variables.

Answer

1. True 2. True 3. False 4. False 5. True

Exercise 3:

Review questions:

Question 1: What is recursion, and how does it differ from iterative solutions?
Question 2: What is the base case in a recursive function, and why is it important?
Question 3: How does Python handle the call stack in recursion?
Question 4: What is tail recursion, and how does it improve performance?
Question 5: Can you name a common problem that is often solved using recursion?
Question 6: What are the essential components of a recursive function?
Question 7: How do you prevent infinite recursion?
Question 8: What is the main disadvantage of using recursion over iteration?
Question 9: How do recursive functions impact memory usage?
Question 10: Can you have multiple base cases in a recursive function?
Question 11: What is mutual recursion, and can you provide an example?
Question 12: How does Python handle recursive depth, and can it be modified?
Question 13: What are some strategies for debugging recursive functions?
Question 14: How would you write a recursive function that handles both positive and negative inputs?
Question 15: Can you explain how memoization can optimize recursive functions?
Question 16: What is a recursive data structure? Provide an example.
Question 17: How do you trace the execution flow in a recursive function?
Question 18: What are some mathematical operations that can be elegantly solved using recursion?
Question 19: Can recursive functions have side effects? If so, is this advisable?
Question 20: What are the advantages of using recursion for algorithmic problem-solving?

Chapter 12

Modules Packages and file handling

let's break down each of these concepts: modules, packages, and file handling in Python.

Modules:

A module in Python is a file containing Python code that defines variables, functions, and classes. Modules help in organizing code into reusable and manageable components. Modules allow you to encapsulate related code together, making it easier to maintain and reuse. To use the code defined in a module, you need to import the module into your program.

A module in Python is a file containing Python code that can define variables, functions, classes, or other constructs. Modules help in organizing code into reusable and manageable components. They allow you to create separate units of functionality and break down your code into smaller, more manageable pieces.

Modules and file handling are critical features that greatly extend the language's capability and facilitate better organization of code. Modules allow for the compartmentalization of code into separate files, each serving a specific purpose, making it easier to manage and maintain large codebases. By using the import statement, these modules can be easily accessed and their functionalities reused across different parts of an application. On the other hand, file handling enables interaction with external files, be they text, CSV, JSON, or other formats. This feature is essential for tasks such as data storage, data analysis, and logging. Through Python's built-in functions for reading and writing files, developers can efficiently manipulate file data without needing to resort to external software. Both modules and file handling are integral to creating robust, scalable, and efficient Python applications.

```
import my_module
print(my_module.greet("Alice"))  # Output: Hello, Alice!
print(my_module.square(3))       # Output: 9
```

12.1 What is Modular Programming?

Modular programming is the practice of segmenting a single, complicated coding task into multiple, simpler, easier-to-manage sub-tasks. We call these subtasks modules. Therefore, we can build a bigger program by assembling different modules that act like building blocks.

Modularizing our code in a big application has a lot of benefits.

Simplification: A module often concentrates on one comparatively small area of the overall problem instead of the full task. We will have a more manageable design problem to think about if we are only concentrating on one module. Program development is now simpler and much less vulnerable to mistakes.

Flexibility: Modules are frequently used to establish conceptual separations between various problem areas. It is less likely that changes to one module would influence other portions of the program if modules are constructed in a fashion that reduces interconnectedness. (We might even be capable of editing a module despite being familiar with the program beyond it.) It increases the likelihood that a group of numerous developers will be able to collaborate on a big project.

Reusability: Functions created in a particular module may be readily accessed by different sections of the assignment (through a suitably established api). As a result, duplicate code is no longer necessary.

Scope: Modules often declare a distinct namespace to prevent identifier clashes in various parts of a program.

In Python, modularization of the code is encouraged through the use of functions, modules, and packages.

Creating a Module:

To create a module, you simply create a **.py** file with the Python code you want to encapsulate. For example, let's create a module named **math_operations.py** that contains some basic math functions:

```
# math_operations.py

def add(a, b):
    return a + b

def subtract(a, b):
```

```
    return a - b

def multiply(a, b):
    return a * b

def divide(a, b):
    return a / b
```

Using a Module:

To use the functions defined in a module, you need to import the module into your program using the **import** statement:

```
# main_program.py

import math_operations

result1 = math_operations.add(5, 3)
result2 = math_operations.subtract(10, 4)

print("Result of addition:", result1)     # Output: Result of addition: 8
print("Result of subtraction:", result2)  # Output: Result of subtraction: 6
```

In this example, the **math_operations** module is imported, and its functions are used by referencing the module name followed by the function name, like **math_operations.add()**.

Importing Specific Functions:

You can also import specific functions from a module to avoid typing the module name each time:

```
# main_program.py

from math_operations import add, subtract

result1 = add(5, 3)
result2 = subtract(10, 4)

print("Result of addition:", result1)     # Output: Result of addition: 8
print("Result of subtraction:", result2)  # Output: Result of subtraction: 6
```

Renaming Imported Modules or Functions:

You can rename an imported module or function using the **as** keyword:

```
# main_program.py

import math_operations as math_ops

result = math_ops.multiply(4, 5)
print("Result of multiplication:", result)  # Output: Result of multiplication: 20
```

12.2 Packages

A package in Python is a collection of related modules grouped together in a directory hierarchy. Packages allow you to further organize your code and create a modular structure. A package is simply a directory containing one or more module files along with an optional __init__.py file.

Here's how you can create and use packages in Python:

Creating a Package:

1. Create a directory with the desired package name.
2. Place your module files inside that directory.
3. Optionally, create an empty __init__.py file in the package directory.

For example, let's create a package named my_package with two modules: module1.py and module2.py.

```
my_package/
│
├── __init__.py
├── module1.py
└── module2.py
```

Defining Modules Inside the Package:

module1.py:

```
def foo():
    return "This is foo from module1"
```

module2.py:

```
def bar():
    return "This is bar from module2"
```

Using Modules from the Package:

You can import modules from the package using dot notation:

```
import my_package.module1
import my_package.module2

print(my_package.module1.foo())  # Output: This is foo from module1
print(my_package.module2.bar())  # Output: This is bar from module2
```

You can also use the **from ... import ...** syntax:

```
from my_package import module1, module2

print(module1.foo())  # Output: This is foo from module1
print(module2.bar())  # Output: This is bar from module2
```

Using Package-Level Imports:

In the **__init__.py** file of the package, you can define imports that will be available when you import the package:

my_package/__init__.py:

```
from .module1 import foo
from .module2 import bar
```

Now you can directly import functions from the package:

```
from my_package import foo, bar

print(foo())  # Output: This is foo from module1
print(bar())  # Output: This is bar from module2
```

Packages are used to create a structured and organized project hierarchy. They allow for better code organization, reusability, and maintenance by grouping related modules together.

12.3 File Handling:

File handling in Python involves working with files on your computer's filesystem. It allows you to read from and write to files, creating, opening, modifying, and closing them as needed.

File handling in Python refers to the process of working with files stored on your computer's filesystem. It involves tasks such as reading from and writing to files, creating and deleting files, and managing file-related operations. Python provides built-in functions and methods that allow you to interact with files and perform various operations on them. File handling is essential for various tasks such as reading and processing data from external files, writing output to files, working with configuration files, handling logs, and more.

Common file handling operations in Python include:

Opening Files: You use the **open()** function to open a file. It takes two arguments: the file name (including the path) and the mode in which you want to open the file (read, write, append, etc.).

Reading Files: You can use methods like **read()**, **readline()**, and **readlines()** to read the content of a file. These methods allow you to read the file's contents as strings or lists of strings.

Reading Methods:

There are different methods for reading content from a file:

read(): Reads the entire content of the file as a single string.

readline(): Reads a single line from the file.

readlines(): Reads all lines from the file and returns a list of lines.

Writing to Files: The **write()** method is used to write content to a file. You typically open the file in write mode (**'w'**) to write new content. If the file already exists, writing in this mode will overwrite its contents.

Writing Methods:

When writing content to a file, you can use the write() method. You can also use the writelines() method to write a list of lines to the file.

Appending to Files: You can open a file in append mode (**'a'**) to add new content at the end of the file, without overwriting the existing content.

Closing Files: After you're done with a file, it's important to close it using the **close()** method. This releases system resources and ensures that changes are saved to the file. Method to close a file, it's recommended to use the **with** statement (**context manager**). The **with** statement ensures that the file is automatically closed when the block is exited, even if an exception occurs.

Using with Statement: The **with** statement (context manager) is recommended for file handling. It automatically handles the opening and closing of the file, ensuring proper resource management.

Exception Handling: When working with files, you should handle exceptions such as **FileNotFoundError** and **PermissionError**. Using **try** and **except** blocks helps your program handle unexpected situations gracefully.

These are some essential aspects of file handling in Python. Understanding these concepts is crucial for effectively working with files, managing resources, and handling exceptions.

Binary Files: In addition to text files, you can work with binary files using the **'b'** mode. This is useful for handling non-text files like images or audio.

File Pointer (Cursor):

Every file has a file pointer, also known as the cursor. It points to the position in the file from where the next read or write operation will occur. After reading or writing, the file pointer moves ahead by the number of bytes read or written. You can manually move the file pointer using the seek() method.

File handling is crucial for reading data from external sources, writing data for storage or transmission, and managing various types of files. It's an important aspect of programming, especially when dealing with real-world data and interactions.

Mode	**Description**
‘r’	Open text file for reading. Raises an I/O error if the file does not exist.
‘r+’	Open the file for reading and writing. Raises an I/O error if the file does not exist.
‘w’	Open the file for writing. Truncates the file if it already exists. Creates a new file if it does not exist.
‘w+’	Open the file for reading and writing. Truncates the file if it already exists. Creates a new file if it does not exist.
‘a’	Open the file for writing. The data being written will be inserted at the end of the file. Creates a new file if it does not exist.
‘a+’	Open the file for reading and writing. The data being written will be inserted at the end of the file. Creates a new file if it does not exist.
‘rb’	Open the file for reading in binary format. Raises an I/O error if the file does not exist.
‘rb+’	Open the file for reading and writing in binary format. Raises an I/O error if the file does not exist.

Mode	Description
‘wb’	Open the file for writing in binary format. Truncates the file if it already exists. Creates a new file if it does not exist.
‘wb+’	Open the file for reading and writing in binary format. Truncates the file if it already exists. Creates a new file if it does not exist.
‘ab’	Open the file for appending in binary format. Inserts data at the end of the file. Creates a new file if it does not exist.
‘ab+’	Open the file for reading and appending in binary format. Inserts data at the end of the file. Creates a new file if it does not exist.

File handling in Python involves working with files on your computer's filesystem. It allows you to read from and write to files, create, open, modify, and close them as needed. Python provides built-in functions and methods for performing various file handling operations.

Here's how to perform common file handling operations in Python:

Opening a File:

To open a file, you use the built-in **open()** function. It takes two arguments: the file path and the mode (read, write, append, etc.).

```
# Opening a file in read mode
file = open('myfile.txt', 'r')
```

Reading from a File:

You can read the content of a file using the **read()** method:

```
content = file.read()
print(content)
file.close()
```

Writing to a File:

To write to a file, you can open it in write mode ('w') and use the **write()** method:

```
file = open('output.txt', 'w')
file.write("Hello, World!")
file.close()
```

Appending to a File:

To append content to an existing file, open it in append mode ('a'):

```
file = open('myfile.txt', 'a')
file.write("\nThis is a new line.")
file.close()
```

Using with Statement (Recommended):

It's recommended to use the **with** statement (context manager) to automatically close the file when you're done. This ensures proper resource management:

```
# Reading from a file using with statement
with open('myfile.txt', 'r') as file:
    content = file.read()
    print(content)

# Writing to a file using with statement
with open('output.txt', 'w') as file:
    file.write("Hello, World!")
```

```
# Appending to a file using with statement
with open('myfile.txt', 'a') as file:
    file.write("\nThis is a new line.")
```

Reading Line by Line:

You can read a file line by line using a loop:

```
with open('myfile.txt', 'r') as file:
    for line in file:
        print(line.strip())  # Strip to remove the newline character
```

File handling is essential for working with external data, configuration files, logs, and more. Remember to properly close files using the **close()** method or by using the **with** statement to ensure that resources are released after use.

The file related methods

The file object provides the following methods to manipulate the files on various operating systems.

SN	Method	Description
1	file.close()	It closes the opened file. The file once closed, it can't be read or write anymore.
2	File.fush()	It flushes the internal buffer.
3	File.fileno()	It returns the file descriptor used by the underlying implementation to request I/O from the OS.
4	File.isatty()	It returns true if the file is connected to a TTY device, otherwise returns false.
5	File.next()	It returns the next line from the file.
6	File.read([size])	It reads the file for the specified size.
7	File.readline([size])	It reads one line from the file and places the file pointer to the beginning of the new line.
8	File.readlines([sizehint])	It returns a list containing all the lines of the file. It reads the file until the EOF occurs using readline() function.
9	File.seek(offset[,from)	It modifies the position of the file pointer to a specified offset with the specified reference.
10	File.tell()	It returns the current position of the file pointer within the file.
11	File.truncate([size])	It truncates the file to the optional specified size.
12	File.write(str)	It writes the specified string to a file
13	File.writelines(seq)	It writes a sequence of the strings to a file.

12.4 Create the new directory

You can create a new directory (folder) in Python using the built-in **os** module. The **os** module provides a variety of functions to interact with the operating system, including creating directories. Here's how you can create a new directory:

```
import os

# Specify the name of the new directory
new_directory = "my_new_directory"

# Check if the directory already exists
if not os.path.exists(new_directory):
    # Create the directory
    os.makedirs(new_directory)
    print(f"Directory '{new_directory}' created successfully.")
else:
```

```
    print(f"Directory '{new_directory}' already exists.")
```

In this example, the **os.makedirs()** function is used to create a new directory named **"my_new_directory"**. Before creating the directory, the code checks if it already exists using **os.path.exists()**. If the directory doesn't exist, **os.makedirs()** is used to create it.

Remember that the **os.makedirs()** function also creates any intermediate directories that are required. For example, if you want to create a directory structure like **"parent_directory/child_directory"**, the function will create both the parent and child directories if they don't exist.

Make sure you have the necessary permissions to create directories in the location you specify.

The getcwd() method

This method returns the current working directory.

The syntax to use the getcwd() method is given below.

Syntax

```
os.getcwd()
```

Example

```
import os
os.getcwd()
```

Output:

'C:\\Users\\MANISH SONI'

Changing the current working directory

The **chdir()** method in Python is a part of the **os** module, which provides various functions for interacting with the operating system. The **chdir()** method is specifically used to change the current working directory to a specified directory path. The current working directory is the directory from which your Python script is currently running.

Syntax

```
os.chdir("new-directory-path")
```

- **os**: This refers to the **os** module that you need to import before using its functions.
- **"new-directory-path"**: This is the path of the directory to which you want to change the current working directory.

Purpose of chdir():

The chdir() method serves the purpose of allowing you to navigate and perform operations within different directories on your computer's filesystem while your Python script is running.

Why Use chdir():

- **File Operations**: If your Python script needs to perform operations (read, write, delete, etc.) on files located in a specific directory, you can use **chdir()** to switch to that directory before performing the operations.
- **Organization**: When working with multiple files located in different directories, using **chdir()** can help keep your code organized and prevent the need for providing full paths every time you access a file.
- **Relative Paths**: Using **chdir()** along with relative paths (paths that are relative to the current working directory) can make your code more portable and easier to maintain across different environments.
- **Module and Package Imports**: In some cases, Python modules or packages might be located in specific directories. Changing the working directory can simplify importing these modules or packages.
- **Data Processing**: If your script processes data stored in different directories, using **chdir()** can help streamline data processing tasks.

It's important to note that while **chdir()** can be useful, using absolute paths (complete paths from the root directory) is often recommended for clarity and to avoid unexpected behavior when working with different directories.

Remember that changing the working directory affects the context in which your script operates, so use it with caution and ensure you understand the consequences.

How to use the **chdir()** method in Python to change the current working directory:

```
import os
# Specify the path of the new directory
new_directory_path = "C:\\Users\\MANISH SONI\\Documents"

# Change the current working directory to the new directory
os.chdir(new_directory_path)
```

```
# Get and display the current working directory
current_directory = os.getcwd()
print("Current working directory:", current_directory)
```
In this example:

The **os** module is imported to use its functions.

The **new_directory_path** variable is set to the desired path of the new directory you want to switch to.

The **os.chdir()** method is used to change the current working directory to the specified path (**new_directory_path**).

The **os.getcwd()** method is then used to get the current working directory and store it in the **current_directory** variable.

Finally, the current working directory is printed using **print()**.

By using the **chdir()** method, you can navigate to different directories in your file system within your Python script. This can be useful when you need to work with files in specific locations.

1 The file related methods

The file object provides the following methods to manipulate the files on various operating systems.

SN	Method	Description
1	file.close()	It closes the opened file. The file once closed, it can't be read or write anymore.
2	File.fush()	It flushes the internal buffer.
3	File.fileno()	It returns the file descriptor used by the underlying implementation to request I/O from the OS.
4	File.isatty()	It returns true if the file is connected to a TTY device, otherwise returns false.
5	File.next()	It returns the next line from the file.
6	File.read([size])	It reads the file for the specified size.
7	File.readline([size])	It reads one line from the file and places the file pointer to the beginning of the new line.
8	File.readlines([sizehint])	It returns a list containing all the lines of the file. It reads the file until the EOF occurs using readline() function.
9	File.seek(offset[,from)	It modifies the position of the file pointer to a specified offset with the specified reference.
10	File.tell()	It returns the current position of the file pointer within the file.
11	File.truncate([size])	It truncates the file to the optional specified size.
12	File.write(str)	It writes the specified string to a file
13	File.writelines(seq)	It writes a sequence of the strings to a file.

12.5 Error and exception handling

Error and exception handling is an essential part of programming, especially in Python, where various types of errors and exceptions can occur during program execution. Understanding how to handle these situations can help you write robust, fault-tolerant code. Here's an overview of the topics within error and exception handling in Python:

Types of Errors

Syntax Errors: Occur when the parser detects an incorrect statement.

Logical Errors: Also known as bugs; occur when the code doesn't perform as intended.

Runtime Errors: Occur during the program's execution and are not syntactically incorrect, commonly known as exceptions.

Basic Exception Handling

try and except Blocks: Basic structure for catching exceptions in Python.

```
try:
  # code that might raise an exception
except SomeException:
```

```
    # code that will run if SomeException is raised
```

Catching Multiple Exceptions: You can catch multiple exceptions in a single except block.

```
try:
    # code
except (SomeException, AnotherException):
    # code
```

Generic except Clause: Catches any exception but is generally not recommended due to its broad nature.

```
try:
    # code
except:
    # code
```

else Clause: Executes if the **try** block doesn't generate an exception.

```
try:
    # code
except SomeException:
    # code
else:
    # code
```

finally Clause: Always runs, whether an exception was raised or not.

Advanced Exception Handling

Raising Exceptions: Using the raise keyword to trigger exceptions manually.

User-defined Exceptions: Creating your own custom exceptions.

Nested Exception Handling: Using multiple try/except blocks to handle exceptions in a nested manner.

Exception Attributes and Methods

args Attribute: To get the arguments passed to the exception.

with_traceback() Method: To set traceback for an exception.

Built-In Exceptions

Common Built-in Exceptions: ValueError, TypeError, IndexError, KeyError, FileNotFoundError, etc.

Exception Chaining

Using from: To chain exceptions and provide context, e.g., raise SomeException from None.

Exception Logging

Using the logging Module: How to log exceptions effectively for debugging purposes.

Exception Best Practices

Don't Suppress Exceptions: Avoid empty except blocks that catch all exceptions but do nothing.

Be Specific: Catch the exceptions you expect, not all exceptions, to avoid masking issues.

Use Built-in Exceptions: Whenever possible, use Python's built-in exceptions rather than creating custom ones.

Real-world Applications

Data Validation: Using exception handling for validating data inputs in applications.

File Operations: Using exception handling to gracefully handle I/O operations.

Network Requests: Handling network-related exceptions in API calls.

Understanding these topics will give you a comprehensive view of error and exception handling in Python, enabling you to write resilient code that can handle unexpected events gracefully.

Summary

The basic read, write, and append operations, Python also provides functionalities for file positioning through methods like **seek()** and **tell()**. The **seek()** method allows you to jump to a particular byte position in the file, and **tell()** gives the current position, which is useful for scenarios where you need more control over which parts of the file to read or write.

Python also facilitates the reading and writing of binary files with modes like **rb** and **wb**, essential for dealing with non-text files such as images or executable programs.

Exception handling plays a critical role in robust file operations, enabling the program to gracefully handle issues like missing files or lack of permissions. This is commonly implemented using **try** and **except** blocks.

The **os** and **shutil** modules provide utilities for file and directory management, allowing you to programmatically create, delete, or move files and directories. This is particularly useful for automating workflows that involve file system operations.

Furthermore, Python's rich ecosystem includes libraries that can be used for more advanced file handling tasks, such as working with compressed files (**gzip**, **zipfile**), connecting to FTP servers (**ftplib**), and even reading and writing to Google Sheets or Excel files (**gspread**, **openpyxl**).

Overall, file handling in Python is a comprehensive and flexible domain, offering a wide range of capabilities from basic to advanced file manipulations, making it a vital skill for many programming tasks.

Exercise 1:

Multiple Choice Questions (MCQs):

Question 1: What does the r+ mode in file handling signify?

a) Read-only mode
b) Write-only mode
c) Read and write mode
d) Append mode

Question 2: Which method reads the entire file content as a string?

a) read()
b) readline()
c) readlines()
d) readfile()

Question 3: Which built-in module is used for high-level file operations like copy and move?

a) os
b) sys
c) shutil
d) fileutil

Question 4: Which method is used to find the current position of the file pointer?

a) tell()
b) seek()
c) locate()
d) find()

Question 5: Which of the following modes opens the file for appending text?

a) w
b) wb
c) a
d) r

Question 6: What is the default mode when opening a file using open()?

a) w
b) wb
c) a
d) r

Question 7: Which function closes an opened file?

a) close()
b) exit()
c) quit()
d) shutdown()

Question 8: What will the following code snippet output?

```
with open("file.txt", "r") as f:
    print(f.closed)
print(f.closed)
```

a) True True
b) False True
c) False False
d) True False

Answer

1. a 2. a 3. c 4. a 5. c 6. d 7. a 8. b

Exercise 2:

True/False Questions:

Question 1: It's mandatory to close a file after opening it with the with statement.
Question 2: The readlines() method reads the entire file content and returns it as a list of strings.
Question 3: Using the w mode to open a file that already exists will overwrite the file
Question 4: The seek() method can only move the file pointer forward, not backward.
Question 5: The os module can be used for reading and writing text and binary files.

Answer

1. False 2. True 3. True 4. False 5. False

Exercise 3:

Review questions:

Question 1: What is a Python module and how is it different from a script?
Question 2: How do you import a Python module?
Question 3: What is the __name__ variable and how is it related to modules?
Question 4: How do you create your own Python package?
Question 5: What is the purpose of the __init__.py file in a package?
Question 6: Can you import specific functions or classes from a module?
Question 7: What does the as keyword do when importing modules?
Question 8: What are relative imports and how are they used in packages?
Question 9: What is the Python Standard Library?
Question 10: How would you list all functions and variables defined in a module?
Question 11: How do you open a file in Python for reading?
Question 12: What are the different file modes available in Python?
Question 13: How do you write to a file in Python?
Question 14: What methods are available for reading from a file?
Question 15: How do you close a file, and why is it important?
Question 16: How do you read and write a JSON file in Python?
Question 17: How do you handle exceptions during file operations?
Question 18: What is the **with** statement and how is it useful in file handling?
Question 19: How do you read a large file line-by-line in Python?
Question 20: How can you move, copy, or delete files using Python?

Chapter 13

Matplotlib

Matplotlib Python

Matplotlib is a widely-used plotting library for the Python programming language. Developed by John Hunter in 2002, it provides an object-oriented API for embedding plots into Python applications, as well as a functional interface for generating a wide variety of static, interactive, and animated visualizations. Matplotlib is often employed in data analysis, scientific computing, and artificial intelligence tasks to create 2D and 3D graphs, bar charts, scatter plots, histograms, and many other types of visualizations.

The library is highly customizable, allowing you to control almost every aspect of a plot, from the size and type of markers to the styling of labels and axes. This flexibility makes it suitable for preparing figures for scientific papers, generating graphs for web applications, or simply exploring data graphically. Matplotlib is often used in combination with other data science libraries like NumPy for numerical computations and Pandas for data manipulation, offering a comprehensive toolkit for analyzing and presenting data.

Matplotlib's design was inspired by MATLAB, and it has grown to become one of the most robust plotting libraries for Python, with a large and active community that continually contributes to its development. Whether you're a beginner wanting to create simple graphs or an experienced data scientist aiming for complex visualizations, Matplotlib provides the tools to achieve that.

Matplotlib is a popular data visualization library in Python that provides a wide range of tools for creating static, animated, and interactive visualizations in various formats. It is widely used for creating charts, plots, graphs, histograms, and other visual representations of data.

Here's a brief overview of Matplotlib and its key features:

13.1 Installation

Matplotlib is not included in the Python standard library, so you need to install it using the following command:

pip install matplotlib

A matplotlib is an open-source Python library which used to plot the graphs. It is originally conceived by the **John D. Hunter** in **2002**. The version was released in 2003, and the latest version is released 3.1.1 on 1 July 2019.

It represents the data through the graphical form. The graphical form can be a Scatter Plot, Bar Graph, Histogram, Area Plot, Pie Plot, etc. The matplotlib library is generally used to data visualization. Data visualization allows us to make a effective decision for organization.

Let's see the installation of the matplotlib.

Installing the matplotlib

Before working with the matplotlib library, we need to install it in out Python environment. Let's see the following method of installing matplotlib library.

Using Anaconda distribution of Python

The Anaconda distribution is an easiest way to install matplotlib library because matplotlib is pre-installed in it. So we don't need to further installation.

Go to its official site and click the download button.

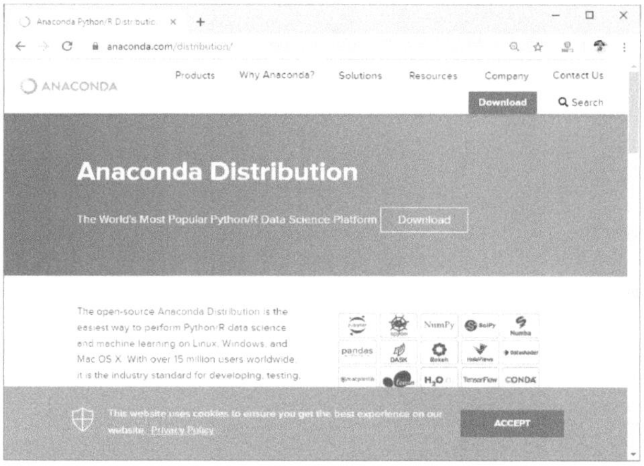

Select the download the version according to your Python interpreter configuration.

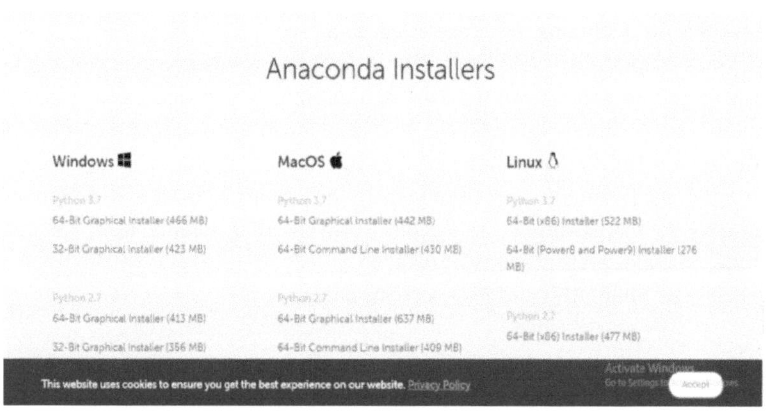

Using pip command

The pip can also use to install the matplotlib library. Open the command prompt, type the following command.

```
pip install matplotlib
```

Confirm the Installation

To verify that matplotlib is installed properly or not, type the following command includes calling .__version __ in the terminal.

```
import matplotlib
matplotlib.__version__
'3.1.1'
```

Now, we are ready to work with the matplotlib.

Basic Example: Here's a simple example of how to create a basic line plot using Matplotlib:

```
import matplotlib.pyplot as plt

# Sample data
x = [1, 2, 3, 4, 5]
y = [10, 15, 7, 12, 9]

# Create a line plot
plt.plot(x, y)

# Add labels and title
plt.xlabel('X-axis')
plt.ylabel('Y-axis')
plt.title('Simple Line Plot')
```

```
# Display the plot
plt.show()
```

Key Features:

- **Easy to Use**: Matplotlib provides a simple and intuitive interface for creating various types of plots and visualizations.
- **Wide Range of Plots**: It supports a variety of plot types, including line plots, scatter plots, bar plots, histograms, pie charts, and more.
- **Customization**: You can customize almost every aspect of your plots, including colors, styles, labels, markers, legends, and annotations.
- **Multiple Axes**: Matplotlib allows you to create multiple axes within a single figure, enabling you to create complex layouts of subplots.
- **Data Visualization**: It is widely used for visualizing data from various sources, such as CSV files, databases, and data manipulation libraries like Pandas.
- **Publication-Quality Plots**: Matplotlib's plots are highly customizable and suitable for creating publication-quality figures for research papers, reports, and presentations.
- **Interactive Visualizations**: Matplotlib can be combined with other libraries like **mplcursors**, **matplotlib.widgets**, and more to create interactive plots.
- **Integration**: Matplotlib can be used in various GUI frameworks, such as Tkinter, Qt, and Jupyter notebooks.
- **3D Plots**: Matplotlib also supports 3D plotting for visualizing 3D data and surfaces.

Matplotlib provides a lot of flexibility, but it may require some learning to master all its features. Additionally, there are other libraries built on top of Matplotlib, such as Seaborn and Plotly, which offer even more advanced visualizations and styles.

13.2 matplotlib.pyplot in Python

matplotlib.pyplot is a submodule of the **matplotlib** library in Python, which provides a convenient interface for creating various types of plots and visualizations. It's a powerful tool for generating graphs, charts, and other visual representations of data.

Here's a basic example of how to use **matplotlib.pyplot** to create a simple line plot:

```
import matplotlib.pyplot as plt

# Sample data
x = [1, 2, 3, 4, 5]
y = [2, 4, 6, 8, 10]

# Create a line plot
plt.plot(x, y, marker='o', linestyle='-', color='b', label='Data')

# Add labels and title
plt.xlabel('X-axis')
plt.ylabel('Y-axis')
plt.title('Simple Line Plot')

# Add a legend
plt.legend()

# Show the plot
plt.show()
```

In this example, **plt.plot()** is used to create the line plot. The **marker** parameter specifies the marker style for data points, the **linestyle** parameter specifies the line style, and the **color** parameter sets the color of the line and markers. The **label** parameter is used to label the plot for the legend.

Other types of plots, such as scatter plots, bar plots, histograms, and more, can be created using different functions provided by **matplotlib.pyplot**.

Remember to install **matplotlib** if you haven't already:

```
pip install matplotlib
```

ou can refer to the official **matplotlib** documentation for more information and examples: https://matplotlib.org/stable/contents.html
Matplotlib Lines, grid, subplot, bars, pieschat, histogram
Matplotlib is one of the most commonly used tools for plotting in Python.

13.3 Line plots, pie chart, histograms, bar and scatter plots

Line plots

So, let's get started with the line plot.

Matplotlib is one of the most commonly used tools for plotting in Python. In this article, we'll look at how to use matplotlib to create some basic plots, such as line plots, pie chart, histograms, bar and scatter plots.

So, let's get started with the line plot.

Line Plot with Grid:

This example demonstrates how to create a simple line plot with grid lines using **plt.plot()**.
x and **y** are lists of data points representing the x and y coordinates of the points on the plot.
The **marker** parameter specifies marker style for data points, **linestyle** sets the line style, and **color** sets the color of the line and markers.
plt.xlabel() and **plt.ylabel()** set labels for the x and y axes, and **plt.title()** sets the title of the plot.
plt.grid(True) adds grid lines to the plot.
plt.legend() adds a legend to the plot based on the **label** provided in **plt.plot()**.
plt.show() displays the plot.

```
import pandas as pd
import matplotlib.pyplot as plt

#number of ice creams sold during a week
ice_cream = [35,33,65,44,75,88,101]

plt.plot(ice_cream)

plt.show()
```

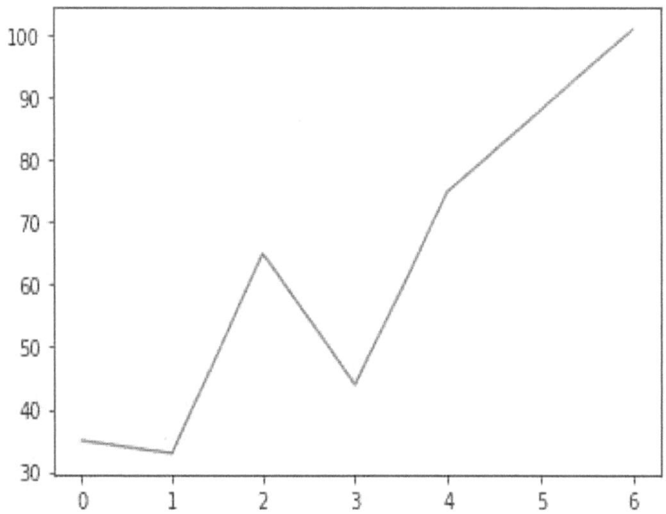

Pie Chart

This example shows how to create a pie chart using **plt.pie()**.
labels contains the labels for each segment of the pie chart, and **sizes** contains the corresponding sizes or values.
plt.pie() generates the pie chart, and **autopct** formats the displayed percentages.
plt.axis('equal') ensures that the pie chart is circular.
plt.title() sets the title of the pie chart.
plt.show() displays the pie chart.

Example

```
x = [64.73,18.43,3.37,3.36,10.11]
labels = ['Chrome', 'Safari', 'Edge', 'Firefox', 'Others']

plt.pie(x, labels=labels,autopct='%.1f%%')
plt.show()
```

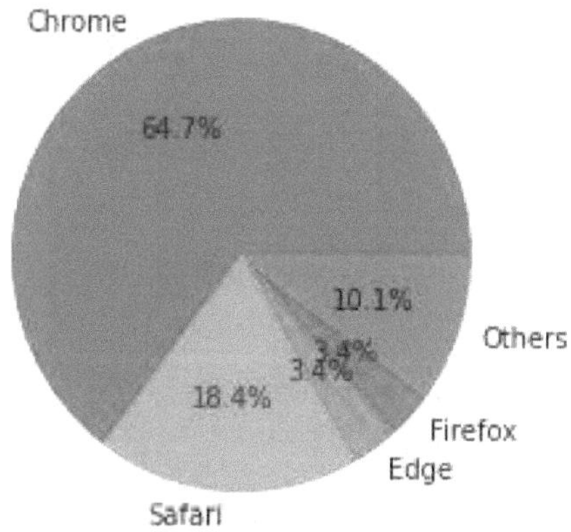

When creating a pie chart using the plt.pie() function in matplotlib, you have the option to visually separate the individual slices by using the explode parameter. The explode parameter accepts a list of values that determine how much each slice should be "exploded" or offset from the center of the pie. This can be useful for highlighting specific slices or creating a more visually distinct pie chart.

Example

```
plt.pie(x, labels=labels,autopct='%.1f%%',explode=[0.1]*5)
plt.show()
```

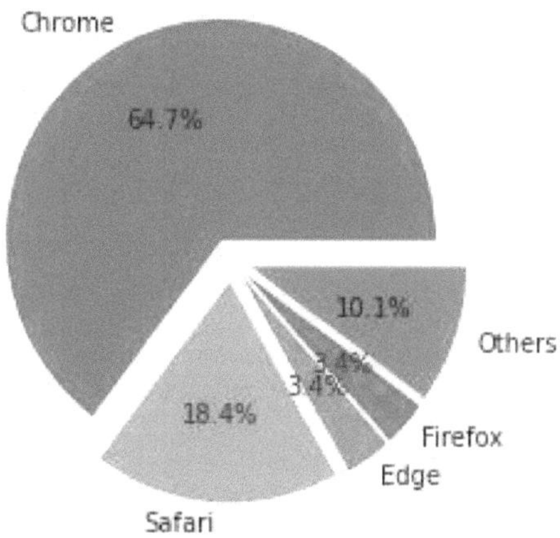

In scenarios where you want to emphasize the market share of a particular category in a pie chart, like highlighting the market share of the "Safari" browser within a web browser market share analysis, you can leverage the **explode** parameter available in the **plt.pie()** function of **matplotlib**. It's important to mention that the length of the **explode** list should match the number of categories in the pie chart.

Example

```
plt.pie(x, labels=labels,autopct='%.1f%%',explode=[0,0.3,0,0,0])
plt.show()
```

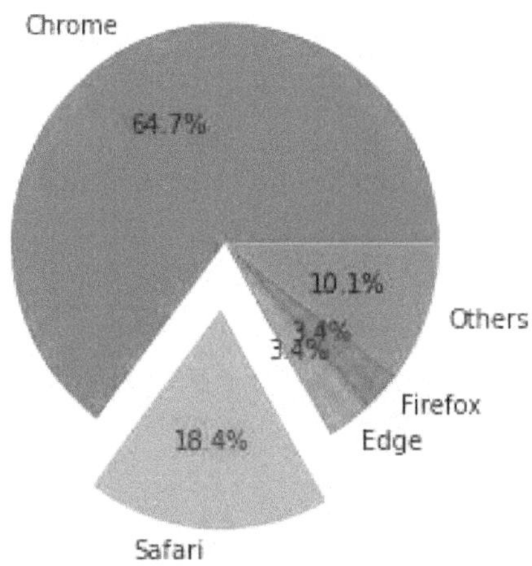

Bar Plot

Let's dive into the details of creating a bar plot using matplotlib.pyplot in Python.

Bar Plot: A bar plot (also known as a bar chart or bar graph) is a graphical representation of data using rectangular bars. Each bar represents a category, and the height or length of the bar corresponds to the value or frequency of that category.

Creating a Bar Plot: Here's a step-by-step explanation of how to create a bar plot using matplotlib.pyplot:

Importing Libraries: First, you need to import the necessary libraries. You'll need matplotlib.pyplot for creating plots and optionally numpy for data manipulation.

```
import matplotlib.pyplot as plt
```

Preparing Data: You'll need data for the categories (x-axis) and their corresponding values (y-axis) to create the bar plot. These can be provided as lists or arrays.

```
categories = ['Category A', 'Category B', 'Category C', 'Category D']
values = [25, 40, 15, 30]
```

Creating the Bar Plot: Use the **plt.bar()** function to create the bar plot. This function takes the categories and values as arguments.

```
plt.bar(categories, values)
```

Customizing the Plot: You can customize various aspects of the plot using different **plt** functions:

Labels and Title: Set labels for the x and y axes and give your plot a title.

```
plt.xlabel('Categories')
plt.ylabel('Values')
plt.title('Bar Plot Example')
```

Colors: You can specify the color of the bars using the **color** parameter.

```
plt.bar(categories, values, color='blue')
```

Width: You can adjust the width of the bars using the **width** parameter.

```
plt.bar(categories, values, width=0.5)
```

Displaying the Plot: After customizing the plot, use **plt.show()** to display it.

```
plt.show()
```

Putting it All Together: Here's the complete code for creating a basic bar plot:

```
import pandas as pd
import matplotlib.pyplot as plt

ice_cream = [35,33,65,44,75,88,101]
days = ['Mon','Tues','Wed','Thur','Fri','Sat','Sun']

plt.bar(days, ice_cream)
plt.show()
```

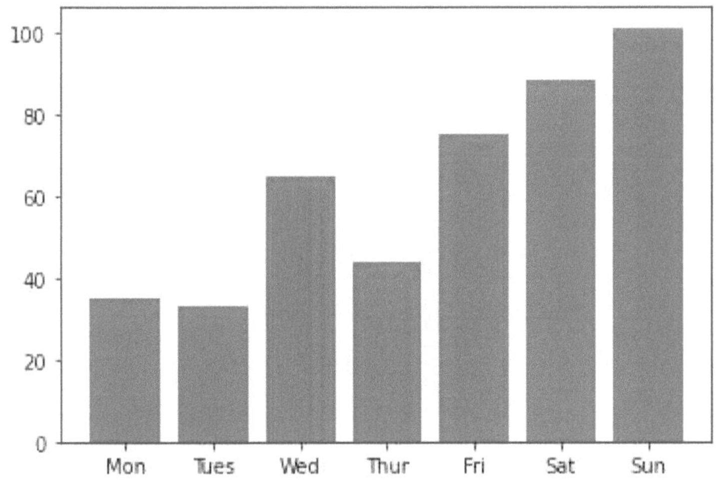

This code will generate a bar plot with four categories and their corresponding values. You can further customize the plot by exploring additional parameters provided by **plt.bar()** and other functions from **matplotlib.pyplot**

To plot a horizontal bar graph we can use the barh() function.

```
plt.barh(days, ice_cream)
plt.show()
```

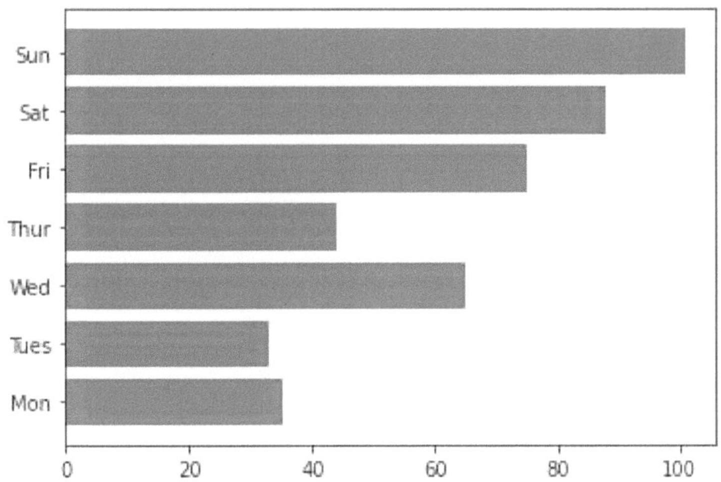

Histogram

A histogram is a visual representation that illustrates the distribution of a set of data points across specified ranges. In simpler terms, it's a chart that displays how often different values or ranges of values occur in a given dataset. For instance, if you collect the heights of 250 individuals, a histogram could help you visualize how many people fall into various height categories To make a histogram in Matplotlib, the **hist()** function is employed. This function takes an array of numerical data as its input to plot the distribution.

To generate a sample array of 250 data points focused around a mean of 170 with a standard deviation of 10, NumPy's random capabilities can be conveniently utilized.

```
import matplotlib.pyplot as plt
import numpy as np

x= np.random.normal(170, 10, 250)

plt.hist(x)
plt.show()
```

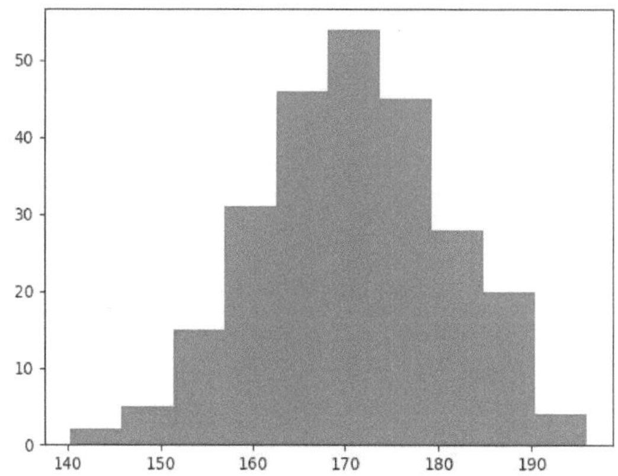

Matplotlib provides a range of different methods to customize histogram. matplotlib.pyplot.hist() function itself provides many attributes with the help of which we can modify a histogram.The hist() function provide a patches object which gives access to the properties of the created objects, using this we can modify the plot according to our will.

Example 1

Python3

```
import matplotlib.pyplot as plt
import numpy as np
from matplotlib import colors
from matplotlib.ticker import PercentFormatter

# Creating dataset
np.random.seed(23685752)
N_points = 10000
n_bins = 20

# Creating distribution
x = np.random.randn(N_points)
y = .8 ** x + np.random.randn(10000) + 25

# Creating histogram
fig, axs = plt.subplots(1, 1,
                        figsize =(10, 7),
                        tight_layout = True)

axs.hist(x, bins = n_bins)

# Show plot
plt.show()
```

Output :

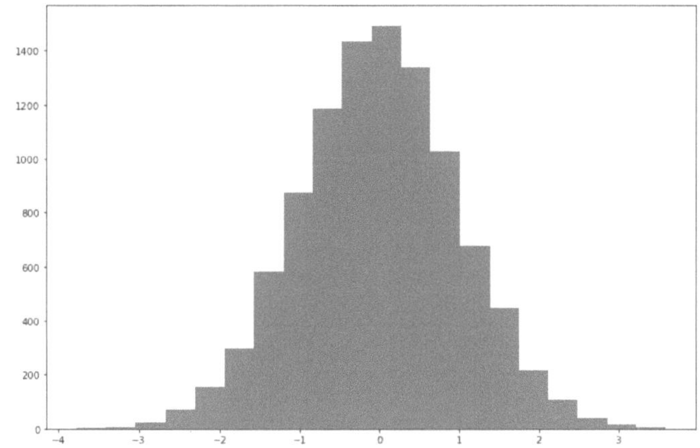

Summary

Matplotlib is a widely-used data visualization library for Python that enables the creation of a variety of charts and plots, including histograms, line graphs, scatter plots, and more. It offers a high level of customization and control over the visual elements, making it possible to produce intricate and publication-quality figures. Originally designed to emulate MATLAB's plotting capabilities, Matplotlib has grown into a comprehensive toolset that integrates well with Python's data science ecosystem, including libraries like NumPy, pandas, and Jupyter notebooks. From simple plots to complex visualizations, Matplotlib serves as a foundational package for visual data representation in Python. Whether you are plotting data for exploratory data analysis, machine learning, or scientific research, Matplotlib offers a range of functionalities to meet varying needs.

In addition to its basic plotting capabilities, Matplotlib excels in rendering a wide variety of graphs, each suitable for different types of data and analysis requirements. These include:

- **Line Graphs**: Ideal for tracking changes over time, line graphs are frequently used in financial analysis and trend identification.
- **Bar Charts**: Useful for comparing quantities across categories, bar charts can be oriented horizontally or vertically.
- **Pie Charts**: Primarily used for displaying proportional representations, pie charts are useful for understanding the composition of a whole.
- **Scatter Plots**: Excellent for correlation and distribution analysis, scatter plots show individual data points on a two-dimensional axis.
- **Histograms**: Suited for understanding the frequency distribution of numerical data, histograms group data into bins and display these as bars.
- **Box Plots**: These are great for identifying outliers and understanding the spread and skewness of your data.
- **Heatmaps**: Used to represent density or intensity of variables, they are often employed in scientific visualizations.
- **Contour Plots**: Useful for showing three-dimensional data in two dimensions, contour plots are often used in geographical data mapping or for visualizing areas of different elevations on a map.
- **3D Graphs**: Although less common due to their complexity, 3D graphs like surface plots and wireframes are available for specific use-cases.
- **Polar Plots**: These are specialized graphs used in mathematics and engineering, particularly for displaying periodic functions.
- **Error Bars**: Often overlaid on line or bar graphs, error bars provide a visual representation of data variability.
- **Time-Series Plots**: Specifically tailored to represent data points at successive time intervals, these are critical in domains like economics and environmental science.

Matplotlib's flexibility allows for the creation of combinations of these graph types, annotations, and custom styling, making it an indispensable tool for anyone looking to understand their data visually.

Exercise 1:

Multiple Choice Questions (MCQs):

Question 1: Which function is commonly used to create a line graph in Matplotlib?

a) bar()
b) plot()
c) scatter()
d) hist()

Question 2: What does the plt.show() function do?

a) Saves the figure
b) Closes the figure
c) Displays the figure
d) Clears the figure

Question 3: Which function is used to create a histogram?

a) bar()
b) plot()
c) scatter()
d) hist()

Question 4: How can you add a title to a Matplotlib plot?

a) plt.title('Your Title')
b) plt.add_title('Your Title')
c) plt.set_title('Your Title')
d) plt.heading('Your Title')

Question 5: Which function is used to create a scatter plot?

a) bar()
b) plot()
c) scatter()
d) hist()

Question 6: How can you save a Matplotlib figure?

a) plt.show('filename.png')
b) plt.save('filename.png')
c) plt.savefig('filename.png')
d) plt.export('filename.png')

Question 7: What is the role of plt.subplot()?

a) Display multiple plots in a single figure
b) Create 3D plots
c) Create subplots within a figure
d) Plot multiple lines on a single axis

Question 8: How do you add a legend to a plot?

a) plt.legend()
b) plt.show_legend()
c) plt.add_legend()
d) plt.set_legend()

Answer

1. b 2. c 3. d 4. a 5. c 6. c 7. c 8. a

Exercise 2:

True/False Questions:

Question 1: The function plt.show() is mandatory to view a Matplotlib plot.

Question 2: Matplotlib can only generate 2D plots and is not capable of creating 3D plots.

Question 3: You can combine multiple types of graphs, like line and bar graphs, in a single Matplotlib figure.

Question 4: The plt.axis() function is used to set the limits of the axes in a Matplotlib plot.

Question 5: Matplotlib is unable to handle real-time data plotting.

Answer

1. True 2. True 3. False 4. False 5. True

Exercise 3:

Review questions:

Question 1: What is Matplotlib, and what is it primarily used for?
Question 2: How do you install Matplotlib?
Question 3: What are the core components of a Matplotlib plot?
Question 4: What is the difference between a figure and an axis in Matplotlib?
Question 5: How do you create a simple line plot?
Question 6: What are some commonly used plot types available in Matplotlib besides line plots?
Question 7: How do you add labels and a title to a plot?
Question 8: What are Matplotlib backends, and why might you change them?
Question 9: How do you save a plot as an image file?
Question 10: How do you customize the line style and markers in a line plot?
Question 11: How do you create multiple subplots in a single figure?
Question 12: What are Matplotlib styles and how can you use them?
Question 13: How do you plot data directly from a Pandas DataFrame?
Question 14: How do you create a histogram using Matplotlib?
Question 15: What is the purpose of the **show()** function?
Question 16: How do you adjust the axis limits for a plot?
Question 17: What are annotations and how can you add them to a plot?
Question 18: How do you create a 3D plot in Matplotlib?
Question 19: What is the **pyplot** interface, and how does it differ from the object-oriented interface?
Question 20: How do you handle real-time data or animations in Matplotlib?

Chapter 14

Python Examples(Important Programs)

Beginners

Here are a few basic Python programs that are suitable for beginners. These examples demonstrate fundamental concepts like variables, input/output, loops, and conditions.

Program 1: Hello, World!

This is the simplest Python program that shows how to print something to the console.

```
print("Hello, World!")
```

Program 2: Adding Two Numbers

This program takes two numbers as input and prints their sum.

```
# Take input from user
num1 = float(input("Enter the first number: "))
num2 = float(input("Enter the second number: "))

# Add numbers
sum = num1 + num2

# Print the sum
print(f"The sum of {num1} and {num2} is {sum}.")
```

Program 3: Even or Odd

This program checks if a number is even or odd.

```
# Take input from user
num = int(input("Enter a number: "))

# Check if number is even or odd
if num % 2 == 0:
   print(f"{num} is even.")
else:
   print(f"{num} is odd.")
```

Program 4: Basic Loop

This program prints numbers from 1 to 10 using a for loop.

```
# Loop from 1 to 10
for i in range(1, 11):
   print(i)
```

Program 5: Basic List Operations

This program demonstrates some basic operations you can do with lists.

```
# Create a list
my_list = [1, 2, 3, 4, 5]

# Print the list
print("Original list:", my_list)

# Add an element to the list
my_list.append(6)
print("After appending:", my_list)
```

```
# Remove an element from the list
my_list.remove(3)
print("After removing:", my_list)

# Access element by index
print("Element at index 2:", my_list[2])
```

These are just simple programs, but understanding them will provide a good foundation for learning more complex topics in Python.

Program 6: Calculate Area of a Circle

Calculate the area of a circle given the radius.

```
import math

radius = float(input("Enter the radius of the circle: "))
area = math.pi * (radius ** 2)
print(f"The area of the circle with radius {radius} is {area}.")
```

Program 7: Reverse a String

Reverse a string entered by the user.

```
text = input("Enter a string: ").lower()
vowels = "aeiou"
num_vowels = sum(1 for char in text if char in vowels)
num_consonants = len(text) - num_vowels
print(f"Vowels: {num_vowels}")
print(f"Consonants: {num_consonants}")
```

Program 8: Count Vowels and Consonants

Count the number of vowels and consonants in a string.

```
text = input("Enter a string: ").lower()
vowels = "aeiou"
num_vowels = sum(1 for char in text if char in vowels)
num_consonants = len(text) - num_vowels
print(f"Vowels: {num_vowels}")
print(f"Consonants: {num_consonants}")
```

Program 9: Simple Interest Calculator

Calculate simple interest based on principal, rate, and time.

```
principal = float(input("Enter the principal amount: "))
rate = float(input("Enter the rate of interest: "))
time = float(input("Enter the time in years: "))

simple_interest = (principal * rate * time) / 100
print(f"Simple Interest: {simple_interest}")
```

Program 10: Print Fibonacci Series

Print the first n numbers in the Fibonacci sequence.

```
n = int(input("Enter the number of Fibonacci numbers to generate: "))
a, b = 0, 1
for _ in range(n):
    print(a, end=' ')
```

```
    a, b = b, a + b
print()
```

Program 11: Factorial of a Number

Calculate the factorial of a given number.

```
n = int(input("Enter a number: "))
factorial = 1

for i in range(1, n + 1):
    factorial *= i

print(f"The factorial of {n} is {factorial}.")
```

Program 12: Find the Largest Number in a List

Find and print the largest number in a list.

```
numbers = [4, 2, 9, 1, 5, 6]
print(f"The largest number is {max(numbers)}.")
```

Program 13: Table of a Number

Print the multiplication table of a given number

```
num = int(input("Enter a number to generate its multiplication table: "))
for i in range(1, 11):
    print(f"{num} x {i} = {num*i}")
```

Program 14: Palindrome Checker

Check if a string is a palindrome.

```
text = input("Enter a string: ")
if text == text[::-1]:
    print(f"{text} is a palindrome.")
else:
    print(f"{text} is not a palindrome.")
```

Program 15: Basic Calculator

Perform addition, subtraction, multiplication, and division based on user input.

```
a = float(input("Enter first number: "))
b = float(input("Enter second number: "))
operation = input("Enter operation (+, -, *, /): ")

if operation == '+':
    print(f"Result: {a + b}")
elif operation == '-':
    print(f"Result: {a - b}")
elif operation == '*':
    print(f"Result: {a * b}")
elif operation == '/':
    if b != 0:
        print(f"Result: {a / b}")
    else:
        print("Error: Division by zero.")
else:
    print("Invalid operation.")
```

Program 16: Find Prime Numbers

This program finds all prime numbers up to a given number.

```
n = int(input("Find primes up to: "))
for num in range(2, n + 1):
    for i in range(2, int(num ** 0.5) + 1):
        if num % i == 0:
            break
    else:
        print(num, end=' ')
print()
```

Program 17: Calculate Average

This program calculates the average of a list of numbers.

```
numbers = [10, 20, 30, 40, 50]
average = sum(numbers) / len(numbers)
print(f"The average of the numbers is {average}.")
```

Program 18: Check Armstrong Number

An Armstrong number is a number that is equal to the sum of its digits each raised to the power of the number of digits.

```
num = int(input("Enter a number: "))
temp = num
sum = 0
n = len(str(num))

while temp > 0:
    digit = temp % 10
    sum += digit ** n
    temp //= 10

if num == sum:
    print(f"{num} is an Armstrong number.")
else:
    print(f"{num} is not an Armstrong number.")
```

Intermediate

These programs demonstrate the use of more advanced concepts like functions, modules, list comprehensions, and dictionaries.

Program 1: Fibonacci Sequence with Memoization

Using memoization to optimize the calculation of Fibonacci numbers.

```
memo = {}

def fib(n):
    if n in memo:
        return memo[n]
    if n <= 1:
        return n
    memo[n] = fib(n-1) + fib(n-2)
    return memo[n]

print(fib(10))
```

Program 2: Calculate Factorial Using Recursion

A recursive function to calculate the factorial of a number.

```
def factorial(n):
    return 1 if n == 0 else n * factorial(n-1)

print(factorial(5))
```

Program 3: Sort a Dictionary by Value

Sorting a dictionary by its values.

```
my_dict = {'a': 3, 'b': 1, 'c': 2}
sorted_dict = {k: v for k, v in sorted(my_dict.items(), key=lambda item: item[1])}
print(sorted_dict)
```

Program 4: Palindrome Checker for Sentences

Check if a sentence is a palindrome, ignoring spaces, case, and punctuation.

```
import re

def is_palindrome(sentence):
    sentence = re.sub(r'[^a-zA-Z0-9]', '', sentence).lower()
    return sentence == sentence[::-1]

print(is_palindrome("A man, a plan, a canal, Panama"))
```

Program 5: Prime Number Checker

Check if a given number is prime or not.

```
def is_prime(n):
    if n <= 1:
        return False
    for i in range(2, int(n ** 0.5) + 1):
        if n % i == 0:
            return False
    return True

print(is_prime(17))
```

Program 6: List Comprehensions

Create a list of squares for numbers in a given range that are even.

```
squares = [x*x for x in range(1, 11) if x % 2 == 0]
print(squares)
```

Program 7: Matrix Transposition

Transpose a given matrix.

```
matrix = [[1, 2, 3], [4, 5, 6], [7, 8, 9]]
transposed = [[row[i] for row in matrix] for i in range(len(matrix[0]))]
print(transposed)
```

Program 8: String Reversal with Stack

Reverse a string using a stack data structure.

```
def reverse_string(s):
    stack = list(s)
    return ''.join([stack.pop() for _ in range(len(stack))])

print(reverse_string("Python"))
```

Program 9: Convert Decimal to Binary

Convert a decimal number to its binary representation.

```
def dec_to_bin(n):
    if n == 0:
        return '0'
    binary = ''
    while n > 0:
        binary = str(n % 2) + binary
        n //= 2
    return binary

print(dec_to_bin(10))
```

Program 10: Caesar Cipher

Encrypt and decrypt text using a simple Caesar cipher.

```
def caesar_cipher(text, shift):
    encrypted_text = ''
    for char in text:
        if char.isalpha():
            offset = ord('A') if char.isupper() else ord('a')
            encrypted_text += chr((ord(char) - offset + shift) % 26 + offset)
        else:
            encrypted_text += char
    return encrypted_text

print(caesar_cipher("Hello, World!", 3))
```

Program 11: Count Word Frequency in a Text File

Count how often each word appears in a text file.

```
from collections import Counter

with open('file.txt', 'r') as f:
    text = f.read()
    words = text.split()
    freq_count = Counter(words)
    print(freq_count)
```

Program 12: Merge Sort Implementation

Implement the Merge Sort algorithm.

```
def merge_sort(arr):
    if len(arr) <= 1:
        return arr

    mid = len(arr) // 2
    left = merge_sort(arr[:mid])
    right = merge_sort(arr[mid:])

    return merge(left, right)

def merge(left, right):
    result = []
    while left and right:
        if left[0] < right[0]:
```

```
            result.append(left.pop(0))
        else:
            result.append(right.pop(0))
    result.extend(left)
    result.extend(right)
    return result

print(merge_sort([5, 2, 9, 1, 5, 6]))
```

Program 13: Anagram Checker
Check if two strings are anagrams of each other.

```
def check_anagram(str1, str2):
    return sorted(str1) == sorted(str2)

print(check_anagram('listen', 'silent'))
```

Program 14: Quick Sort Implementation
Implement the Quick Sort algorithm.

```
def quick_sort(arr):
    if len(arr) <= 1:
        return arr

    pivot = arr[len(arr) // 2]
    left = [x for x in arr if x < pivot]
    middle = [x for x in arr if x == pivot]
    right = [x for x in arr if x > pivot]

    return quick_sort(left) + middle + quick_sort(right)

print(quick_sort([3, 6, 8, 10, 1, 2, 1]))
```

Program 15: Depth-First Search (DFS) in Graph
Implement a Depth-First Search in a Graph represented as an adjacency list.

```
graph = {'A': ['B', 'C', 'E'],
         'B': ['A', 'D', 'E'],
         'C': ['A', 'F', 'G'],
         'D': ['B'],
         'E': ['A', 'B', 'D'],
         'F': ['C'],
         'G': ['C']}

visited = set()

def dfs(visited, graph, node):
    if node not in visited:
        print(node)
        visited.add(node)
        for neighbour in graph[node]:
            dfs(visited, graph, neighbour)

dfs(visited, graph, 'A')
```

Program 16: Linear Search Implementation

Implement a linear search algorithm to find a target value in a list.

```
def linear_search(lst, target):
    for i in range(len(lst)):
        if lst[i] == target:
            return i
    return -1

print(linear_search([1, 2, 3, 4, 5], 3))  # Output will be 2
```

Program 17: Web Scraper for Quotes

Use the requests and BeautifulSoup libraries to scrape quotes from a webpage. You'll need to install the packages if you haven't (pip install requests BeautifulSoup4).

```
import requests
from bs4 import BeautifulSoup

url = "http://quotes.toscrape.com/"
response = requests.get(url)

soup = BeautifulSoup(response.text, 'html.parser')
quotes = soup.find_all("span", {"class": "text"})

for i, quote in enumerate(quotes):
    print(f"Quote {i + 1}: {quote.text}")
```

Program 18: Calculate Mean, Median, and Mode

Calculate the mean, median, and mode of a list of numbers.

```
from collections import Counter

def mean(numbers):
    return sum(numbers) / len(numbers)

def median(numbers):
    numbers.sort()
    middle = len(numbers) // 2
    if len(numbers) % 2 == 0:
        return (numbers[middle - 1] + numbers[middle]) / 2
    else:
        return numbers[middle]

def mode(numbers):
    count = Counter(numbers)
    return [k for k, v in count.items() if v == max(count.values())]

numbers = [1, 2, 3, 4, 4, 4, 5, 5, 6]
print("Mean:", mean(numbers))
print("Median:", median(numbers))
print("Mode:", mode(numbers))
```

Advanced

Below are advanced-level Python programs that span multiple topics including algorithms, machine learning, web development, and more.

Program 1: Binary Search Tree Implementation

```
class Node:
    def __init__(self, key):
        self.left = None
        self.right = None
        self.val = key

def insert(root, key):
    if root is None:
        return Node(key)
    else:
        if root.val < key:
            root.right = insert(root.right, key)
        else:
            root.left = insert(root.left, key)
    return root

def inorder(root):
    return inorder(root.left) + [root.val] + inorder(root.right) if root else []

root = None
root = insert(root, 4)
insert(root, 2)
insert(root, 1)
insert(root, 3)
insert(root, 5)

print(inorder(root))
```

Program 2: Implementing a Stack using LinkedList

```
class Node:
    def __init__(self, data):
        self.data = data
        self.next = None

class Stack:
    def __init__(self):
        self.head = None

    def is_empty(self):
        return self.head is None

    def push(self, data):
        new_node = Node(data)
        new_node.next = self.head
        self.head = new_node

    def pop(self):
        if self.is_empty():
            return None
        temp = self.head
        self.head = self.head.next
        popped = temp.data
```

```
        return popped

# Example usage:
stack = Stack()
stack.push(1)
stack.push(2)
stack.push(3)
print(stack.pop())  # Output: 3
```

Program 3: Dijkstra's Shortest Path Algorithm

```
import heapq

def dijkstra(graph, start):
    distances = {node: float('infinity') for node in graph}
    distances[start] = 0
    queue = [(0, start)]
    while queue:
        current_distance, current_node = heapq.heappop(queue)
        if current_distance > distances[current_node]:
            continue
        for neighbor, weight in graph[current_node].items():
            distance = current_distance + weight
            if distance < distances[neighbor]:
                distances[neighbor] = distance
                heapq.heappush(queue, (distance, neighbor))
    return distances

# Example usage:
graph = {
    'A': {'B': 1, 'C': 4},
    'B': {'A': 1, 'C': 2, 'D': 5},
    'C': {'A': 4, 'B': 2, 'D': 1},
    'D': {'B': 5, 'C': 1}
}
print(dijkstra(graph, 'A'))  # Output: {'A': 0, 'B': 1, 'C': 3, 'D': 4}
```

Program 4: Naive Bayes Classifier from Scratch

```
from collections import defaultdict, Counter
import math

def separate_by_class(dataset):
    separated = defaultdict(list)
    for features, label in dataset:
        separated[label].append(features)
    return separated

def summarize_data(dataset):
    summaries = {}
    for label, instances in dataset.items():
        attribute_summaries = [(attribute, Counter([instance[attribute] for instance in instances]))
                               for attribute in range(len(instances[0]))]
        summaries[label] = attribute_summaries
```

```
    return summaries

def calculate_probability(x, attribute_summary, total_count):
    count_x_given_y = attribute_summary[x] if x in attribute_summary else 0
    p_x_given_y = (count_x_given_y + 1) / (total_count + len(attribute_summary))
    return p_x_given_y

def predict(summaries, instance):
    best_label, best_prob = None, -1
    for label, attribute_summaries in summaries.items():
        p_y = len(attribute_summaries[0][1]) / sum(len(attribute_summary[1]) for attribute_summary in attribute_summaries)
        p = math.log(p_y)
        for i in range(len(instance)):
            attribute, attribute_summary = attribute_summaries[i]
            p += math.log(calculate_probability(instance[attribute], attribute_summary, len(attribute_summary)))
        if best_label is None or p > best_prob:
            best_prob = p
            best_label = label
    return best_label

# Example Usage
dataset = [((1, 0), 'yes'), ((1, 1), 'no'), ((0, 1), 'yes'), ((0, 0), 'no'), ((0, 1), 'yes'), ((1, 1), 'no')]

separated_dataset = separate_by_class(dataset)
summaries = summarize_data(separated_dataset)

new_instance = (1, 0)
print("Predicted label for instance {}: {}".format(new_instance, predict(summaries, new_instance))) # Output: 'yes'
new_instance = (0, 1)
print("Predicted label for instance {}: {}".format(new_instance, predict(summaries, new_instance))) # Output: 'yes'
```

This is a basic example and does not cover many aspects like handling continuous variables or missing data. Also, it uses a Laplace smoother (+1) in the **calculate_probability()** function to handle zero probabilities.

Program 4: Binary Search Tree Implementation

```
class Node:
    def __init__(self, key):
        self.left = None
        self.right = None
        self.val = key

def insert(root, key):
    if root is None:
        return Node(key)
    else:
        if root.val < key:
            root.right = insert(root.right, key)
        else:
            root.left = insert(root.left, key)
    return root

# In-order traversal
```

```
def inorder(root):
    return inorder(root.left) + [root.val] + inorder(root.right) if root else []

root = None
root = insert(root, 50)
insert(root, 30)
insert(root, 70)
insert(root, 20)
insert(root, 40)
print(inorder(root))
```

Program 5: Quick Sort Algorithm

```
def quicksort(arr):
    if len(arr) <= 1:
        return arr
    pivot = arr[len(arr) // 2]
    left = [x for x in arr if x < pivot]
    middle = [x for x in arr if x == pivot]
    right = [x for x in arr if x > pivot]
    return quicksort(left) + middle + quicksort(right)
print(quicksort([3,6,8,10,1,2,1]))
```

Program 6: Linear Regression using scikit-learn

```
from sklearn.linear_model import LinearRegression
import numpy as np

X = np.array([1, 2, 3, 4, 5]).reshape(-1, 1)
y = np.array([2, 4, 3, 3, 5])

model = LinearRegression()
model.fit(X, y)

predictions = model.predict(np.array([6, 7]).reshape(-1, 1))
print(predictions)
```

Program 7: Fibonacci Sequence using Dynamic Programming

```
def fibonacci(n, memo={}):
    if n in memo:
        return memo[n]
    if n <= 2:
        return 1
    memo[n] = fibonacci(n - 1, memo) + fibonacci(n - 2, memo)
    return memo[n]

print(fibonacci(50))
```

Program 8: Web Scraping using BeautifulSoup and requests

```
from bs4 import BeautifulSoup
import requests

response = requests.get('http://www.example.com/')
soup = BeautifulSoup(response.text, 'html.parser')
```

```
# Extract and print all paragraph texts on the page
for p_tag in soup.find_all('p'):
    print(p_tag.get_text())
```

Program 9: RESTful API Server using Flask

```
from flask import Flask, jsonify

app = Flask(__name__)

@app.route('/api', methods=['GET'])
def api():
    return jsonify({"message": "Hello, World!"})

if __name__ == '__main__':
    app.run(debug=True)
```

Program 10: Basic Neural Network using TensorFlow

```
import tensorflow as tf

# Create a simple neural network
model = tf.keras.models.Sequential([
  tf.keras.layers.Dense(10, activation='relu', input_shape=(8,)),
  tf.keras.layers.Dense(1)
])

# Compile the model
model.compile(optimizer='adam',
              loss='mean_squared_error')

# Some sample data (8 features, 1 label)
X = np.random.rand(100, 8)
y = 3*X[:, 0] + 2*X[:, 1] + 4*X[:, 2]  # Just an example relation

# Fit the model
model.fit(X, y, epochs=100)

# Make a prediction
print(model.predict(np.random.rand(1, 8)))
```

Before running these programs, make sure to install the required libraries using pip (pip install scikit-learn tensorflow flask requests beautifulsoup4). These are advanced programs that use external libraries and modules. They also demonstrate the application of Python in various domains like machine learning, web development, and dynamic programming.

Sample Videos

Topic	Link	QR Code
Introduction to Python	https://youtu.be/GStOTKCp84s	
Python Interview	https://www.youtube.com/playlist?list=PLzlh_31VWEFo6d1LKrcGSoNk20AJPIcl0	